WRITING JUVENILE FICTION

Books by Phyllis A. Whitney

Adult Novels

THUNDER HEIGHTS
THE MOONFLOWER
SKYE CAMERON
THE TREMBLING HILLS
THE QUICKSILVER POOL
RED IS FOR MURDER

Novels for Young People

CREOLE HOLIDAY
THE FIRE AND THE GOLD
THE HIGHEST DREAM
A LONG TIME COMING
STEP TO THE MUSIC
LOVE ME, LOVE ME NOT
LINDA'S HOMECOMING
EVER AFTER
WILLOW HILL
THE SILVER INKWELL
A WINDOW FOR JULIE
A STAR FOR GINNY
A PLACE FOR ANN

Mysteries for Young People

SECRET OF THE SAMURAI SWORD
MYSTERY OF THE GREEN CAT
MYSTERY ON THE ISLE OF SKYE
MYSTERY OF THE BLACK DIAMONDS
THE ISLAND OF DARK WOODS
MYSTERY OF THE GULLS

Textbook

WRITING JUVENILE FICTION

PHYLLIS A. WHITNEY

Writing

Juvenile Fiction

BOSTON

THE WRITER, INC.

Publishers

CONTENTS

Chapter

Introduction to the Revised Edition

One of the things a writer has no time for is the reading of his own books after they are published. This one has been no exception, so when my editor asked if it should be revised before bringing out a new edition, I approached it with the curiosity one might feel in picking up a book by a stranger.

The first edition of *Writing Juvenile Fiction,* published in 1947, was based on a background of six books, several hundred short stories, some teaching at Northwestern University and at several writers' conferences, and several years as the Children's Book Review Editor of a metropolitan daily. Since that time, twenty more books, ten more years of teaching at New York University, more writers' conferences, and much involvement with the manuscripts of aspiring writers have kept me too busy really to examine this book with a critical eye. For this reason I wondered what my reaction would be on a rereading. Had its tenets held over the years? Would it still seem sound?

It was pleasing to discover that further experience, particularly in working with other writers, confirmed the advice offered in its pages. Apparently these are methods and techniques which stand the test of time and which student writers can apply successfully to their own work.

The chapter on specialization has been completely rewritten. There was more to be said on this matter, and the categories themselves could now be expanded and made more useful in the light of recent trends. Most other changes have been in the interest of presenting new policies and developments in the juvenile field. None of the fundamental principles has been reversed or struck out.

There is one thing about *Writing Juvenile Fiction* that leaves me unhappy. That is the word "juvenile" in the title. In many ways this word has come to have a faintly patronizing implication. The word "children" would be a happier word, and "young people" even better. But "children" does not include the teen-agers, and "young people" may not seem to include children of picture book age. Unfortunately, "juvenile" is the only word we can find that covers the entire range—so that word must remain in the title as this is a book about writing for all these ages.

During the years since it was first published, it has brought me many gratifying experiences. It is wonderfully warming to receive a letter from a stranger who feels that the book has helped straighten out some puzzling problem, or has aided him toward publication. Most of all, it is satisfying when readers tell me that my words have given them the courage to keep trying. If this new edition continues to do these things, the author and publisher can ask no greater satisfaction.

—PHYLLIS A. WHITNEY

WRITING JUVENILE FICTION

I

WHY WRITE FOR CHILDREN?

One of the first lessons the writer of young people's stories and books must learn is a hard one. However bravely and hopefully he sets out, however much he may respect his audience and believe in the worth and importance of what he is doing, he will find almost at once that his efforts, whether published or not, will be looked upon with condescension by his friends, by other writers, in fact by anyone who is not actively concerned with children.

Make no mistake about it, this attitude, until you become immune to it, can sting. It is one of the penalties you will have to pay in return for the many rewards which come to those who write for children. Apparently the general idea seems to be that after a while you will "grow up" and turn out something respectable and dignified and important like an adult novel.

Finally, to prove I could do it, I wrote a "grownup" book. It was a murder mystery, and, if the reviewers were right, not too bad a job. After it was published a well-meaning lady came up to me one day.

"I understand you've written a mystery novel," she said. I admitted that I had.

"It's a grownup book, isn't it?" she persisted.

Again I admitted the unhappy truth.

She nodded approvingly. "Isn't that fine! You're going ahead now. One of these days you'll be writing something *significant*."

I decided that the next time I looked about for a victim for a murder mystery, I would make this woman my first choice. Since that time I have written a number of adult novels, but I know I will never want to leave the juvenile field. Whatever of "significance" I may write is done for young people.

The mystery-romances I write for the adult market are fun in a different way, but they are also very hard work. I find, however, that it rests me to turn from one field to another and that I have less inclination to go stale if I can find variety in my writing. Of course in the adult book market there is always the possibility that one may reach the best-seller list, perhaps serialization, here or abroad, perhaps selection by one of the book clubs. There are greater limitations on earnings in the juvenile field, but there are also special rewards, and the possibility of larger steady earnings.

Since you who are reading this book are contemplating a career in writing for children, let's have a look at some of these rewards and find out how worth while they are.

Perhaps the greatest of all is the satisfaction of writing for an audience still plastic in character. Too often with adults the pattern is so firmly set after twenty that you can do very little about it. Give a grownup a book concerning some controversial subject and what reaction are you likely to get? If the book agrees with what he believes, he will tell you it is a good book. If it disagrees, he'll tell you how bad it is. But the chances are that his opinions are so jelled that he will resist any effort to change them. It isn't that his plight is hopeless and he can't change, but rather that as people grow older they are inclined to cling more and more lovingly to accustomed ruts of thinking, so that anything short of a devastating upheaval will not pry them loose from an opinion, however antiquated. Fortunately, this is not true of all adults. Unfortunately, it is true of the greater majority.

With young people the plasticity, the flexibility has not yet been lost. Wrong thinking today may be changed sometimes overnight for right thinking tomorrow. One of the most touching things about youth is its eagerness to improve, to learn the better way and how to apply it to everyday conduct. The occurrences which happen to an admired hero or heroine, the lessons they learn, the sympathetic struggle these story-book characters make to become the sort of person every youngster would like to be, can sometimes have a lasting effect on the boy or girl who reads the story. The writer for this audience has his reward over and over again in his sense of contributing something to the mental and emotional well-being of the children who read his stories.

He has too, or should have, an almost frightening sense of responsibility. Writing for children is not something to approach lightly and blithely, with no regard for the effect of your words upon your readers. But, fortunately, if that is your attitude, you will probably not be published, for guardians stand all about in this field: editors, librarians, teachers, booksellers, parents. What may get past one, will undoubtedly be caught by another. As a writer, you may feel at times that you are hemmed in by unreasonable restrictions and taboos. After all, you read your story out loud to Johnny Jones and his gang and you know they loved every word of it. It is ridiculous that some stuffy grownup should have the nerve to tell you that your story might not be good for young readers. What you have probably overlooked is that Johnny Jones would also love to fly upside down in an airplane, drive an automobile at eighty miles an hour, and play with loaded firearms. Maybe you'd better bow to a few restrictions for the time being and grant the right of guardianship to those more versed in child psychology than you may be.

So much for the spiritual rewards. Now for the commercial side. I'm afraid I have little patience with the writer who writes only to please himself. I know a number of such "artists" and their so-called idealism leaves me cold. If you have nothing to give that the world wants to read, what good are you as a writer? A writer must be read to be worth his salt, and it is quite likely that if no one wants to read what you write, you and not the world may be in the wrong.

It is also necessary in our kind of world to earn a living, and it is admirable enough to want that living to be the best we can possibly make it and still retain our integrity. In no field of writing are the monetary rewards likely to be immediately sufficient. Don't, whatever you do, give up all else upon receiving your first check and set out to earn your way by writing. A great many people earn a very good living by writing alone, but earning ability comes slowly, as it does in any other vocation. You must establish yourself, become known in your field, find regular markets where you can repeat with more sales, and perhaps find ways of supplementing the income you earn from your fiction.

You will not find that the checks which eventually replace those little printed slips will compare notably with the glittering sums paid by slick paper magazines. Nor will your book sales at best rival the numbers run up by current best-selling adult novels.

The picture, however, has its comforting side. The competition in the juvenile writing field, while not to be scorned, is nothing to the competition for those impressive slick paper checks. The chances for the beginner to break in are fair enough if he has something to give. The editors are kindly and ready to help, and there are a number of extremely low-paying markets in the religious publication group where you can at least have the satisfaction of breaking into print while you are learning.

In the book field the picture is encouraging. Book markets are legion and editors are eager to discover the new writer who shows real promise. Your returns in the book field may not rate with the nearest best-seller, but few books become best-sellers anyway, compared to the number published in a year. The average juvenile is almost sure to pile up more impressive sales than the average, non-best-selling novel. Your adult novel is sadly short-lived. Three months, four months, rarely more than six, and the sales drop to nothing, the book goes out of print. But the juvenile book, while it may not pile up sales spectacularly in the first months of publication, goes quietly on selling year after year, earning the author a steady income. Put a few books behind you and the earnings increase from year to year, even during droughts when no new book is published. Juvenile books are kept in print far longer than adult novels and are apt to go into edition after edition as the years run on. It is not at all uncommon to hear from some writer of juveniles that a book he had published eighteen or twenty years before is still bringing him royalties.

Quite often an adult novel by an unknown writer will stop with a sale of under 5000 copies. The 10% royalty on a $3.50 book which sells 4000 copies is $700.00—not an overwhelming sum to receive for the months of work which may go into the writing of a novel.

In the children's field, even the longest book is likely to run no more than 50,000 words, which falls below average novel length. Depending on the age group for which you are writing, the wordage may drop below that—from the 30,000-word book, to the picture book of 1,000 words or less. Thus the time involved in writing a juvenile (providing you have properly trained yourself in nose-to-the-grindstone habits) is much less than it would take to write an adult book. And the chances are good that you will sell at least 4,000 copies of the longer length selling at $3.00 a copy. If the book is well received, so that the libraries keep wearing out copies, it may go on selling for years, running the total to 10,000 and up.

For the younger age the sales can run to quite breathtaking figures, though the book may sell for less and a cut may go to the artist; all factors which pare down royalties earned for the author.

Taking a look at the over-all picture, one must recognize that earnings in the juvenile writing field are not likely to purchase yachts and Hollywood swimming pools in any great hurry. If you train yourself to be a steady producer, if you so organize your working time that you make the best of whatever hours you can arrange for writing, you can earn a modest income. As you become established you can run that income up to a respectable figure, depending on your own ability and ingenuity.

Probably, however, if you have a real bent for writing for children, you will not consider these things first. You will be likely to react as do the artists who produce the beautiful illustrations now to be found in children's books. Any artist will tell you that illustrating children's books is not particularly lucrative when you compare the sums paid by publishers with those paid in the commercial advertising field. Yet children's books never want for the best of art work.

People who take part in the illustrating and making of children's books do so because they love to do it. Because they find in the work a satisfaction that may not be completely tangible, but which is there, nevertheless, and which causes them to give the best of themselves to the work, even when it sometimes means passing up larger checks.

So you, too, will write for children because that is what you want to do, because that is what you most enjoy doing. You will turn a deaf ear to the people who ask when you are going to write that "grownup book." You will suffer the usual rejection slip fever, the discouragement and disappointment that are part of the beginner's lot. You will stay with your appointed task grimly and doggedly, until the awkwardness of using new tools wears off, and one exciting day you take into your hands a magazine carrying your first printed story, or you unwrap from its brown paper a copy of your first book. Some weeks or months later a child writes you a letter, or tells you in person that he thought your story was "swell." And you wouldn't change places for anything in the world with the author of this year's grownup bestseller.

II

Let's Talk About You

We have been talking about the pros and cons of writing for children. Now let's talk about you, the writer. What are your qualifications? What are your assets and handicaps? What have you to bring to this particular field of writing? Or to any field of writing?

Perhaps you are not yet sure whether you want to specialize in writing for children. That's all right, too. It is just as wise in the beginning to shop around and try your hand at various types of writing until you have found your rightful and comfortable niche. One word of warning—don't take up writing for young people because it looks easy and you mean to use it as a training ground to get somewhere else.

This type of writing is a specialist's job. It is not easy and it will require the very best you can give it. When you have served your apprenticeship in the juvenile field, you will have learned *how to write for children*. You will not have learned how to write for the pulps, or the slicks, or to write adventure or detective or love stories. True, there is some overlapping. A great many rules and much that can be said about writing habits in general will apply to all kinds of writing. But if you intend to use writing for children as a stepping-stone, you would be better off serving your apprenticeship in the field for which you want to write. Writing for children will not spoil you for any other kind of writing, but neither will it prepare you for tossing off stories which you hope will appear in *The Saturday Evening Post,* or *The Atlantic Monthly.* If you still want to write for those markets, then you will have to spend some time learning how to write for them. So have your fling at various types if you are not sure where you belong, but when you find the kind of writing which best suits you, stay with it. Don't pick some other type because it appears to be an easy short-cut. Those first glances can be pretty deceptive.

Let's have a look first of all at some of the qualities you will need to have (or to develop) if you are going to be any kind of a writer.

How is your vitamin content? Because you're going to need energy, energy, energy. Not perhaps the kind of energy it takes to dig a ditch, or win a game of ping-pong, but energy nevertheless. There are times when a hard stint of sitting at a typewriter will leave you as fagged, mentally and physically, as if you had put in a day at hard labor. I remember writing a twelve-page chapter about an exciting basketball game and doing it all at one sitting. When I got up from my desk I was as limp with weariness as if I had actually made every play in that game personally.

Nevertheless, this is the type of energy that even invalids can sometimes manage. Robert Louis Stevenson is only one of the many writers who achieved a prodigious output in spite of ill health. And I have known individuals who bounced with good health, and still could not take the grind of sitting at a typewriter because it so tired them.

Next, how is your courage? Perhaps the major requirement of a writer is the kind of backbone that never gives up, the kind of chin that can take it—not once, but again and again. If you pride yourself on your "sensitivity," if you curl up and die when some brute expresses a low opinion of your brain child, if you get your feelings hurt easily—well, I won't say you can't be a writer. But I certainly will say that you won't be a very good one until you take yourself in hand and toughen up. You can, you know. Nobody has to be like that.

What are these things you'll have to learn to take? Rejection slips of course. So what if your first three masterpieces don't sell? What if your first thirty don't? Or what if you sell one story with ease, and after that you write nothing but failures for months? Can you keep going back to your typewriter? Can you hang on with the kind of grim determination that will not be beaten?

I am sure I can point to a great many writers (myself among them) who started out with more determination than talent. And I can point to brilliant flash-in-the-pan writers who haven't the ability to plod and stick with it through the inevitable discouragement. They fall by the wayside, while the rest of us who may not really write as well, keep ourselves to a steady course until we eventually learn how.

In my own case it took me four years from the time I first mailed out a story to an editor to make my first sale. In three more years I sold three more stories. That adds up to seven years and four stories sold. Can you take it to that extent? Let me add, by way of comfort, that you probably won't have to. I am an unusually horrible example, and if I were a centipede I couldn't have gotten off on more wrong feet.

It is all very well to have your eye on a star, but much

wiser to keep your feet moving step by step along the path that leads to the star, instead of trying to make it all in one jump. When you find out the type of writing you most want to do, don't start out by taking aim at the top market in that field. That is a waste of time, unless you're a genius. If you're the latter you won't be reading this book because you'll know all about it without my help. But if you're just an ordinary guy or gal who wants to write salable stories, have a try at the less glittering markets which may possibly be interested in your stuff while you're in the process of learning your craft. You're not ready for that spotlight act and probably won't be for a while.

Let's say you have energy, courage, determination. Patience is another quality you'll need. Patience to take endless pains over small details. Patience to re-write. Patience to wait. Just plain patience.

Next, how are you when it comes to budgeting your time? Oh, so *that's* your trouble! You are full of energy, courage, determination and patience, but you simply do not have any time. Your head is filled with story ideas, and some day you are going to get them down on paper. Some day when you have time.

You are just the person I want to talk to. It may surprise you to know that nobody else has any time either. Look at successful people in any line of work and you'll find that the thing they have less and less of with every passing year is time.

Time is not something you "have." It is not even something you "find." It is something you *make*. You make it forcibly by pushing other things out of the way. Other things you want to do; even other things you ought to do.

Yes, I know. You work all day in an office. You're all worn out when you come home at night. By the time dinner's over there really isn't any time. And on Saturday you have to wash clothes, or wash the car, or do the marketing. And on Sunday—well, you have to have some fun, don't you?

Or you don't work in an office. You are a housewife. Anybody knows that keeping house is a full-time job. And besides, there are the children. How can anybody write with kids running around, getting into trouble, getting hurt, getting sick, asking questions? After all, your job as a mother comes first. When the baby is a little older, perhaps; or when Johnny gets started to school. . . .

Don't fool yourself. If you belong to the I-haven't-got-time category, you'll never have time. The office job will keep taking more and more out of you, the children will prove more difficult as they grow older, and when the current reasons for not having time run out, you'll be able to find plenty of new ones, all equally logical and impressive. There's your emotional state, for instance. Have you tried that? With all these dreadful things going on you are simply too upset to write. This works in connection with anything, from the news in today's paper, to the fact that your husband didn't kiss you good-bye when he went to work this morning.

The kids have a word for it. That word is "nuts!" If you want to write, you'll make time. If you don't want to, you'll manage to rationalize yourself out of really getting to it.

I know plenty of writers, both men and women, who work all day and still manage to make time to write. And sell what they write. Every one of them hopes to reach that happy state where writing will earn more than the job, so that they can give up the job and "have time to write." Meanwhile, they are doing a wonderful budgeting of whatever time they can make—whether it means getting up an hour earlier in the morning, or sitting inside all day on Sunday, or fitting in an hour at the typewriter every night.

I know women who write straight through having babies, and afterwards, while the children are growing up. Instead of doing the housework early in the morning as a good housewife should, perhaps they have to turn their hand to that at four o'clock in the afternoon. They, too, dream of the day when they'll "have time." In the meantime they are busy making it, and those checks that come in take care of Johnny's tonsils, or buy Susy's new shoes, and sometimes they even buy the writer an Easter bonnet.

Then, at what the story writers used to call "long last," the time comes when these industrious little workers begin to make their writing pay. Oh, happy day! The news that he is losing a valued employee is broken to the boss. Somebody is hired to scrub the floors. Isn't this jolly? Now we're really going to *have* time to write!

Are we? Don't be funny.

Take me again. The same horrible example I told you about. I can live by my writing now. I can give my whole day to it. My daughter is away at school till after three o'clock. The housework is off my hands. But I hope you don't think I really have time to write this book? As a matter of fact, I haven't any business attempting it. I'm only doing it because I remember so well all those years when editors wouldn't pay any attention to me, and now when an editor asks something of me, I'm still so pleased I can never bring myself to say anything but "yes."

I won't weary you with an account of all the writing jobs I happen to be carrying right this minute. I am only one of many doing this. A little success brings more work, and more work means less time, and so it goes. So—I *make* time. More about that later, but for the moment, don't talk to me about being too busy to write. I will yawn and say, "You don't really want to."

Now that we have disposed of a few general qualities you will need as a writer, suppose we get down to one very special quality you will require if you mean to write for young people. Perhaps we might call it the ability to remember.

If you are a woman, what happens when you see two or three teen-age girls putting their heads together in public? You watch a while. You see them whisper and giggle and all talk at the same time. You see them go suddenly off into peals of laughter surely out of all proportion to the cause. How do you react? Do you think, "Gracious, what idiots!" Or do you think, "I remember. . . . Once I was like that," and watching those girls you can recapture how it feels.

Or if you're a man and you see some boys clowning and shoving each other around, maybe showing off a little, do you see them with impatient objectivity, or can you remember what it was like to be that way yourself?

If you're writing for the in-between ages, can you feel the excitement and interest you want your young readers to feel? Does that stone Johnny has just turned up look like a dirty old rock to you, or can you understand how wonderful it seems to young eyes that have never beheld a stone quite so remarkable before? Or if you want to write for the very youngest, can you look at a tree or a toad, a house, a worm, a city sidewalk, and catch the wonder and excitement that object has to the fresh, inexperienced eyes of the littlest ones?

When it comes to emotion, can you understand with your own feelings what a tragic occurrence the loss of a favorite marble can be? Can you write about Mary Jane, who hasn't a dress to wear to a dance, and sense the deep hurt this may cause your young heroine?

A great many people really cannot remember how it feels to be young. Those people should certainly never attempt to write for children. If, however, you can regard the tragedies of youth with a sympathy and understanding that do not discount their importance, yet which bring to them the leavening quality of your more mature years and experience, then you have something worth while to contribute as a writer. It is not a type of writing to which you can come carelessly and empty-handed, wondering only what you will get out of it.

III

WHERE DO YOU BELONG?

Now that we have discussed the why's of writing for children, and the qualities, general and specific, needed by the writer, we are ready to break the field into age groups and find out where you, the individual writer, belong.

Perhaps you already know exactly the age for which you want to write. In that case, one problem is simplified. Many writers, however, do not in the beginning have any particular bent toward one age group. It may even be that you haven't considered "age groups." "Writing for children" covers the whole subject as far as you are concerned and it may dismay you to find that you must now choose a specified group and keep within the limitations of writing for that group.

If you are undecided, try your hand at writing for different ages, until you find the age with which you are most in sympathy and for which you write best.

In my reviewing of children's books I have found it advisable to break the ages roughly into four groups: 2-6, 6-8, 8-12, 12 up. The boundaries for these groups are not by any means fixed and there is a great deal of overlapping. A ten-year-old may sit herself down most contentedly with an "easy" book, only to be found the next day with her nose in a book "for 12 up." The six-to-eights often enjoy picture books intended for younger children. It all depends on the reading ability, tastes and day-to-day inclination of the individual child.

Nevertheless, it is necessary for the sake of bewildered parents, and others who cannot always read the book before giving it to a child, to arrange some age grouping. This grouping will also be of value to you as a writer, since it will enable you to slant your stories with special intent. If other ages also enjoy what you have written, that is fine, but they will not be your direct concern while you are writing for your chosen market.

Each group has certain advantages and disadvantages which concern the writer. Each has its individual problems, and the writer who can comfortably turn out stories for the teens may find himself completely baffled by the picture book technique. Suppose we consider these four groups in order and find out what some of their problems are.

PICTURE BOOKS—2-6

It is a constant thorn-in-the-side to writers for the older ages that picture books often sell in overwhelmingly greater numbers than books which take much longer to write. In the magazine field, where the writer is paid by the word, the author of stories for the very young (which may run about 300 words, depending on the requirements of each magazine) earns considerably less than the one who turns out a 3,500 word story. But in the book field the earnings of the picture-book writer may completely eclipse the earnings of those who write for older young people.

The author of books for the teens learns with anguish that some little book of twenty pages and a few dozen words has sold 30,000 copies in a few months, while his own volume of

60,000 words has taken a year to climb to a sale of 5,000. Perhaps he sniffs scornfully and remarks that he ought to give up writing "real" books and get into the "racket."

Fine. Let him try it! As a rule he doesn't, of course, because writing those few dozen words may be completely beyond his power. I am quick to admit that it would be beyond mine. It isn't so easy as it looks. However, *you* may be the one who can do it. If you are, the field is a lucrative one.

We can treat the writing of material for the youngest, whether for magazine or book market, as almost the same thing. Sometimes the brief book manuscript gets by on a poorer story, carried to success by the illustrations. For the magazine, the story must be good enough to stand on its own feet.

A story for young people of any age must be written for one or more of several reasons. It *must* entertain. It might be wise for you to print that rule in big letters and tack it up over your desk. Check every story you write against it. If it isn't entertaining, into the wastebasket with it. Other reasons which may motivate your writing of a story are to teach a lesson, or to present information. But never forget for one moment that your young reader does not in the least give a hoot about learning lessons or being informed. If he picks up your story or book it is because he wants to be entertained, not preached at. In presenting the manuscript of "Of Human Bondage" to the Library of Congress, Somerset Maugham said, "Fiction is an art;" its purpose "not to instruct, but to please." Well might that be taken for a motto by writers in every field.

However, you may not write your story with your attention wholly upon your young reader. Him you *must* entertain, but there are all those guardians you have to consider as well. It is the adult who buys the book for the child. Editors know this and they know that certain things make an immediate appeal to the grownup. The child may look only for entertainment, but the adult who buys expects something more. Since it is to the editor (and the adult buyer) that you must sell your story, you as a writer will be wise if you put other ingredients into your writing besides the first one of entertainment value.

You may, as I have said, slip into your story a worthwhile lesson, or some interesting information. But remember—*slip* it in. If it sticks out all over your story, like the bumps on a giant's club, your reader will immediately suspect that somebody is trying to teach him something and that, as far as he is concerned, will be the end of you as a story teller. Gone are the days (praise be) when every story ended: "And so, dear children, you must never, never tell a fib, or you too may fall down a well and get all drowned like poor little Percival."

Today the child psychologist will tell you about such things as "fear complexes." You'd better know something about them if you're going to write for the very young. No threats, mind you. No dreadful disasters befalling some defenseless storybook character who is only making the same mistakes every child makes. You may want to help your young reader to be truthful, or kind, or courageous, or any of a number of other virtues, but you are not going to frighten him into it with threats.

One of my favorite lesson-teaching picture books of some years ago is *Charcoal* by Lloyd Coe. Children eight years old and older enjoy this charming book as much as the very young. The lesson comes pretty close to sticking out, but it is so engagingly and entertainingly presented that children fall in love with the book on sight. Like the best of children's books it is one which grownups, too, enjoy, and as far as I am concerned it rates with *Ferdinand* in quality. It has more point to it than *Ferdinand* and the pictures are just as funny.

Charcoal is a black sheep. Because he is a black sheep everyone expects him to be naughty. (That's one in the eye for grownups who will have to read the story out loud over and over and might just as well be learning a little parent-psychology along the way.) Because everybody expects him to be naughty, of course he is, and one of the naughtiest things he does is to push his white sheep cousins into some prickly blackberry bushes.

But in spite of enjoying his naughty tricks, Charcoal always feels lonely and unhappy afterwards. Finally he decides that it must be his black color that makes him naughty, so he finds some whitewash and rolls in it. Now he knows he won't have any more black-sheep thoughts, but will be a very good little white sheep.

Then he happens to see two of his cousins standing near the blackberry bushes. "Swoosh!" go his good intentions and he pushes the cousins right into the bushes! Apparently color hasn't anything to do with being good after all.

Just about that time a storm comes up and three frightened little rabbits run to him to plead for shelter. Charcoal crouches over them, even though the rain comes down and washes away the whitewash. The other sheep look out from the shelter of the woods and see Charcoal doing something so kind that they are very proud of him. So the little black sheep discovers the happy feeling you can have inside after doing something good and he likes it much better than the unhappy feeling he used to have after doing something naughty. After that, he keeps on "doing good things and hardly any bad ones for the next fourteen years."

Here the psychology is sound and no impossible standard of conduct is held up at the end of the story. The fact that Charcoal from then on does "hardly any" bad things is a master touch. Lloyd Coe is fortunate enough to be his own artist and the pictures are as good as the story.

About the time *Charcoal* was published, another picture book of the same type came to me to review, and I could not help but draw a comparison between the right way to present a lesson and one that is psychologically unsound and may actually have an ill effect on some children.

The second book was about a chameleon who got a bit "biggety." But instead of being punished for his rudeness and his overly fine opinion of himself by losing his friends and feeling unhappy inside, he lost his tail. That is dangerous, frightening symbolism. All children are sometimes rude and to give them stories which threaten physical mutilation as punishment for bad behavior may cause the beginning of serious fears.

In this connection I would like to quote from an article by Naoma Zimmerman which appeared in *The Writer,* April 1946, on writing for the preschool child. In fact, I feel that anyone interested in writing for this age should make a point of reading all of what Mrs. Zimmerman has to say in her piece.

"Much of the child's thinking and feeling takes place in terms of unconscious symbolism. This is reflected in the kind of stories which children themselves improvise; it is also in terms of such symbolism that they interpret the stories which they hear. Children readily identify *themselves* with characters in stories—regardless of whether the characters are people, animals, or even inanimate objects. Children love stories which articulate and dramatize their own inner struggles and conflicts. They are fascinated by 'The Gingerbread Boy' because his running away symbolizes their own wish to defy and outwit authority. Unfortunately, the symbolism in the story gets warped and distorted in the end—for the Gingerbread Boy met with a singular fate (for one who was endowed with human characteristics) —he was devoured by the fox. The child interprets the symbolism something like this: 'If you rebel, or even have secret thoughts of rebellion, you are courting some kind of vague punishment or danger.' Anxieties are stirred and the child feels uneasy. If instead of threatening disaster, this story had somehow conveyed the impression that feelings of rebellion are quite natural and understandable—but even so, parents and home are mighty comforting, despite the inconveniences and annoyances, then it would have helped the child to articulate his conflict and resolve it in a *satisfying* and *realistic* way.

". . . To be avoided at all cost is any kind of symbolism which arouses fear of bodily mutilation. Children can take stories of giant-killing with complete equanimity—for giants and killings are sufficiently remote. But stories in which characters suffer from, or are threatened with injury or loss of anatomical parts, strike deep into the child's existing fears of mutilation. Monkeys without tails, strange things happening to people's ears or noses, all have a decidely unwholesome effect on the small child. I know these stories have a fatal fascination for children, but so would a loaded gun."

A writer who has reached an outstanding position with her books for younger children is Ruth Krauss. One of her earlier books still remains a great favorite. Its worth is perennial. In *The Growing Story,* the author tells about a little boy and the four seasons. In the beginning he and his puppy and some chicks are very little. With the coming of spring the little boy puts his warm winter clothes away in a box and goes outside to play. As the days grow longer everything begins to grow. The grass, the flowers, the leaves. Even the puppy and the chicks. Through summer and autumn this growth is quite visible to the little boy. But the little boy cannot see that he is growing at all.

Then winter comes and he takes down the box with his warm clothes and puts them on. And what do you think— the coat is too tight, the sleeves are too short!

Such a story goes to *where the child is* and tells him just what it will comfort him to know. No moral is superimposed from outside. The author has considered the child's needs in writing her story and the book is worth studying for the simplicity and effectiveness of the treatment.

A deservedly popular book for this same age is *A Little House of Your Own* by Beatrice Schenk de Regniers. There is no real story here—it is the elaboration of an imaginative idea familiar to all children. While it's fun to be with grown-ups and with other children, sometimes it is nice to have a little house of your own. Almost anything can make a house for a small child. Under the dining room table, under an umbrella, or beneath a quilt, can all make wonderful houses. The delightful pictures by Irene Haas carry out the idea and the whole book is one to be treasured.

This element of leaving the very young reader satisfied

psychologically is not to be overlooked. Two picture books which do this to perfection are *The Little Fisherman* and *The Little Fireman* by Margaret Wise Brown. In these stories there is a big fisherman and a little fisherman, a big fireman and a little fireman. The little ones can do everything the big ones can, but they do everything on a smaller scale. Except that the big fireman dreams a little dream, while the little fireman dreams a GREAT BIG DREAM. Don't attempt to copy this particular technique, but study these books in order to understand the effect they have upon the children who read them with so much pleasure.

Munro Leaf's lessons in manners are an example of how not to put across a moral. Not that Munro Leaf doesn't get away with it in part, since children seem to enjoy his funny pictures and even swallow the lessons with amazingly good grace. But there is nothing subtle about this method and the result which might be gained is often lost when some misguided adult dashes for the book at a moment of crisis and shrills, "There you are! See! You're a Sulker, just like the picture!" Or a Wriggler, a Food-Waster, a Noisy, or any other of the dozens of categories most children fit into at one time or another in their lives. The child so admonished is likely to achieve a hatred for that particular book which makes it completely ineffective.

Sometimes the purpose behind a picture book may be to provide information. A glimpse of another country or a special section of our own country may be given. Or the picture book may lead the reader back into history. Sometimes it merely deals with the familiar—a grocery store, a circus, a zoo, and so on.

In writing for the very young the trick of repeating certain words or phrases throughout the story is an effective one. Marie Hall Ets has used repetition most successfully in *In the Forest*. Here the technique of telling is unusual since the story of the little boy's walk in the forest is told in the first person. The "I" of the story goes for a walk and meets a great number of imaginary animals who accompany him until a grownup appears on the scene, when they all vanish. The phrase which becomes a rhythmic refrain is "when I went for a walk in the forest." This is a truly delightful picture book and can be studied to good effect.

The picture book which tells no story at all, but gives factual material in an entertaining manner is enormously popular these days. Non-fiction is somewhat outside the province of this book, but your library will give you examples of hundreds of books about everything from seashells to dinosaurs. Or information may be given in the background of a story and be equally effective. You have the world and all that's in it to draw on for such material.

Another category which is enormously popular these days is what we might call the everyday-experience picture book. Alvin Tresselt is a master of this type of book, as you will find in his *I Saw the Sea Coming In* and others. *A Tree is Nice*, by Janice May Udry, won a Caldecott award with Marc Simont's beautiful pictures of what a tree can mean to a child.

One of the difficulties of writing for the picture-book age lies of course in the matter of getting suitable art work for your story. The writer for older children sends in his story and the publisher assigns it to an artist, if one is wanted. But what about the writer who wants to work with the age where pictures are as important as the story? What does he do about an artist?

The answer is that the picture book story must be good enough to stand on its own feet. If it is worth publishing, you can count on the juvenile book editor's imagination to visualize possibilities. The editor knows a great deal more about this than most writers do. She will have in mind a certain format and size, a certain number of pages. If you try, without professional experience, to do this work for her, it may handicap your story.

Of course if you know an accomplished artist who wants to try a finished picture and a few roughs to accompany your story, that may be to your advantage. Even then, a completely finished product isn't required, since the editor will prefer a free hand.

As a beginner in this field you cannot afford to pay the artist ahead of time yourself. You may promise him a share of the royalties if the book sells, but I would not advise going farther than that. He must be willing to take the gamble with you.

Of course if you yourself are an artist, and can write your own picture book stories, you can reap a very nice profit in this field, since you'll split royalties only with yourself. Leo Politi, Louis Slobodkin, Crockett Johnson and many others manage this combination successfully. However, be sure you learn how to tell a good story or you will not find a market, no matter how wonderful your drawings.

If your picture book story is accepted and an artist is assigned to it by the editor, you will be expected to give him a share of your royalties, as arranged for by contract. If a good deal of art work is needed, 50-50 may be a fair arrangement. A name artist may have the feeling that he has done the lion's share of the work, and the author may have to take a smaller share—40-60 perhaps. But don't forget that if it were not for those few lines of story the book would not exist for him to illustrate. Of course the ideal way is to leave the matter of art work to the editor and accept whatever arrangement can then be worked out. But *first* you have to interest the editor—and I believe that is where we came in.

SIX TO EIGHT

This group is perhaps less of a pattern than any other. It will contain picture books with longer stories which the beginner may read for himself. Or it may contain "harder" stories which must be read aloud to him.

There has been a good deal of campaigning in recent years for "graded" words. That is, it was felt that in writing for younger children a special vocabulary list was necessary. Of course in the picture book group words should be kept fairly simple, but if the *right* word happens to be a big word, I feel that it should be used.

I recommend to anyone who means to write for young people Annis Duff's *Bequest of Wings*. It is a book about one family's adventures in reading and it is rich treasure trove for those interested in writing for children. In the chapter called "Fun With Words," Mrs. Duff has this to say:

"I believed then, and I believe even more firmly now, *that all words belong to children*. They choose them for their own use by the simple process of taking possession of the ones they need to express what they want to say. If children do not hear speech that has variety and liveliness, and if their books do not have unfamiliar words tucked in like bright little surprises among the everyday ones, how in the world are they ever to accumulate a store of language to draw on, as new experiences and sensations increase the need and desire to communicate with the people they live with? Children, like the rest of us, need to be articulate, and it seems to me a withholding of what is properly theirs, to limit their choice of words (as in the 'vocabulary-tested' book) to the vocabulary already possessed by an 'average' child of any given age."

A word of warning might be added here for the writer, however. A great many beginners have a tendency to display their erudition, or indulge in what they regard as "fine" writing by tossing around many-syllabled words, where the simple word would be more to the point and more effective. Let's not take the fun of meeting new words out of children's reading, but on the other hand let us not write so that an interpreter is needed for every other sentence.

In writing for the six-to-eight group the rule of interest first still holds good and the lesson must be less simple and obvious. Information may become more complex and all sorts of interesting matters may be presented in story form. But remember always that you are telling a story and that however fascinating and important you feel the educational side of your work may be, it must always be warp and woof of the story itself, and not superimposed. At the upper range of this age bracket, stories can be longer and the plots fairly complex.

A writer whose books for this age are especially good is Miriam E. Mason. *Susannah, the Pioneer Cow* is one of her best. The book has a decided emotional appeal for children and the picture of covered-wagon days is skillfully presented in story guise.

However, the most popular type of story in this age group is the story which deals realistically with modern children and their problems. If you have a special sympathy for this age and an interest in its everyday problems, this may be the right place for you. Again, these books depend heavily on pictures, but the problem of providing illustrations is the editor's. Make your story sufficiently good and worthwhile and the publisher will find the right artist to illustrate it. With longer stories, the artist will probably be paid by the publisher. However, if there are a good many pictures and a name artist is used, the author may be asked to share a percentage of royalties with the artist.

Sometimes a specialty helps with this age. Lee Wyndham has had a fine success with her books about the little dancer, Susie. There is *A Dance for Susie, Susie and the Dancing Cat* and a number of other titles, all dealing with a little girl who is studying ballet. The dancing information is sound, as the author has written a number of books about ballet, both fiction and non-fiction, for older readers. But there is a well-plotted story besides to hold the interest, and excellent characterization. An unusual touch with these Susie books is that the young heroine is a little older with each book and the reader can follow her as she grows as a dancer.

Helen Kay is an extremely gifted writer for this age, with a special understanding and sympathy for children. *The Magic Mitt*, a satisfying story of a little boy who couldn't learn to catch, grew out of an experience in her own family, and is particularly well liked by boys. *A Pony for the Winter* delights the hearts of little girls who dream of the wonderful experience of owning a pony, even temporarily. Again you will find a sound story.

Wee Joseph by William MacKeller, the winner of a citation from The Child Study Association, is a moving story of a little Scottish boy who needs a miracle to save his doomed puppy. And don't miss the stories of Carolyn Haywood, with their fascinating use of everyday details. Days in school, vacation time, shopping with mother—all these and many other matters provide the very best of story material.

Your own library will give you further titles and the librarian will help you discover books which deal effectively with current problems and are liked by young readers.

I am going to say this more than once and I might as well begin now: *Make the problem in your story one that will really interest children.* Keep your own adult interests out of it unless you want to write for adults. I remember a manuscript once submitted to me in a class in which the hero's story problem was to earn enough money to buy books for school. Laudable, indeed, but can you imagine any youngster getting excited about such a project? To buy a bicycle—ah! Or any one of hundreds of other things a boy might like. But out of all the things there are under the sun, this author had to pick school books!

EIGHT TO TWELVE

This age is really fun to write for. There is apparently a greater market for stories for this group than for almost any other. Most young people's magazines are interested in publishing stories for this age and book publishers never seem to get enough. Certainly libraries are always crying for more.

Now there are fewer limitations, and plot comes into its own. Illustrations may still be used, but they are subordinate to the story—mere frosting on the cake. However, a new division begins to appear. For younger children you don't have to think much about writing for boys or girls, but now there is a choice to make. Girls will read boys' books, so if you make your leading character a boy, you will probably reach everyone. But if you want to write about a girl you must resign yourself to having your audience cut in half. Boys miss a lot of good stories because of this snooty attitude, but there seems to be little to do about it. Probably the matter will be settled for you automatically. Some women can write boys' stories, others cannot. I have no choice in the matter because I will never be able to write from the viewpoint of a boy character. I'm afraid he would sound awfully sissy. There are always boys in my stories, but I don't get into their shoes while I'm writing about them. Perhaps if I had a son instead of a daughter I might be able to manage it, but as it stands my interest lies decidedly in the girls' field.

A point to remember in writing for this group is that children like to read about characters who are older than themselves, or at least as old, so don't make your main character too young.

I'd like to recommend a few writers who are particularly successful in writing for this "in-between" age. Even though you may prefer to write the shorter length, these books are worth studying to see how the authors get their excellent effects. One thing they all have in common. It is one of the most important ingredients of fiction writing: emotional effect. Each of these books will make you *feel:*

The *Betsy-Tacy* books, by Maud Hart Lovelace
The Hundred Dresses (and other titles as well),
 by Eleanor Estes

The Melendy Family, by Elizabeth Enright
Roller Skates, by Ruth Sawyer
Ballet Shoes, by Noel Streatfeild
Sizzling Pan Ranch, by Lee Wyndham
Here Come the Clowns!, by Celeste Edell
Homer Price, by Robert McCloskey
Journey Cake, by Isabel McLennan McMeekin
Jump Shy, by Joan Houston
Bronko, by Rosa Eichelberger
The Lost Ones, by Robert Shaffer
Sawdust in His Shoes, by Eloise Jarvis McGraw

This list could run on for columns more, but if you will read these few books, you will have learned a great deal about telling a story which carries real appeal for children. The list doesn't presume to be a list of the "best" books ever published. It is merely a list of book titles about which the youngsters who come and go in our house say, "This is a *good* book."

TWELVE AND UP

Last of all, we have the "twelve and up" group. Many of these books are read by ten-and-eleven-year-olds, but it is simpler to refer to the teen-agers. There is also a new category of books for "young adults," which may deal with youthful problems at a more adult and perceptive level. The books of Mary Stolz are an example of this trend. But for the most part young people of 12-13-14 read these books and you need to confine yourself to their interests. This doesn't mean that your main character may not be grown up and out of school. What happens when they finish high school and college interests this age tremendously. Of course if your book happens to have the quality of universality, its appeal is unlimited, and older readers will find it out for themselves. Books like *Treasure Island* and *Little Women* are ageless.

This is the most difficult age to write for because these books are every bit as hard to do competently as a full-length adult novel.

Here, again, there is a need to choose whether you are going to write for boys or girls. Among the leaders in the boys' group are John Tunis, Gilbert Douglas, Jim Kjelgaard, Howard Pease, Stephen W. Meader, Glen Rounds, Philip Harkins, Jackson Scholtz, Walter Farley and others.

In the girls' field you will find the names of Mary Stolz, Florence Crannell Means, Betty Cavanna, Anne Emery, Harriett Carr, Amelia Elizabeth Walden and many more. If you have something of excellence to produce in the teen-age field, there is surely a place for you.

None of these listings of titles and authors is intended to be comprehensive. When you decide on the age group for which you want to write, go to the library and read everything you can lay your hands on in that field, good and bad alike. In fact, pay particular attention to the books you do not like, in order to note wherein they fail. Then you can avoid the same pitfalls.

In turn, each of these age groups can be broken into many different types of stories and you may in the end want to specialize. It may prove worth while to you to become known as a writer of airplane stories, sports stories, school, career, or almost any other special type of story. But we will consider these specialties later.

IV

WORKING HABITS

Beginnings are important. Sometimes they are dangerous. If your first successful story is written with your left hand, using an onyx pen and green ink while flying in a plane over South America, you may have a real problem on your hands. Forever after, you may think you can write successful stories only with your left hand, using an onyx pen and green ink, while flying in a plane over South America.

You think that sounds extravagant? It isn't very. I have known writers who have clung persistently to the weirdest, most inconvenient writing habits, simply because a story written under such conditions happened to click. I remember one writer of my acquaintance who had to do his early writing while traveling around the country, living in hotels. Hotel desks never suited him and he contrived some sort of back-breaking arrangement whereby he set his typewriter on a chair and himself on a pile of phone books. Later, when he had his own home and a comfortable desk and chair, he still thought he could not write until he got his machine on a chair and himself on a pile of phone books on the floor. It took a lot of reconditioning before he was cured.

I knew another man who had a pair of "writing pants." His despairing wife gave them away to the ragman one day and as a result a career was blasted for months.

Of course it's silly. Of course you will do nothing like that. But you'd better watch yourself with a hawk eye in the beginning, until satisfactory writing habits are so ingrained that you don't have to worry. You may get the idea that you can write only with a certain pencil, or on a certain kind of paper. Or you may decide that you can't possibly start work each morning until after the mailman comes. Or you have to tidy your entire desk—you could never work looking at a mess like that. Or you have to sharpen pencils, pick lint off the floor, or feed the goldfish and water all the plants.

When these very common symptoms begin to appear, get them in hand at once. If you don't, they'll rule you and waste your time. In this matter you are not dealing simply with your conscious self. You're dealing with a subconscious imp who is a lazy fellow. He knows that once you get to that typewriter he is going to be chained down and forced to work, and he will do everything possible to resist that—until you get him trained. This same imp, once he is harnessed, can be your most valued assistant, but he has to be shown who is boss.

So you start out by telling him that at nine o'clock in the morning, or at seven at night, or whenever it is that you can write, you are going to sit down and start writing. When that time comes, you do exactly that. You resist all the wonderful distractions with which the imp will supply you at that time, and you start to work. If you give in to him, you'll be sorry because he can condition you to failure just as easily as you can condition him to working. If, day after day, you fiddle away your working period at odd jobs that ought to be done at some other hour, then you will develop the habit of being a procrastinator instead of a working writer. But the conditioning can work just as easily the other way if you are persistent. You can train that subconscious imp to such stern working habits that when the appointed time comes each day, he will give in without a struggle and turn himself to helping, instead of hindering you. Once you get him on your side you can use him in a lot of ways I'll tell you about from time to time.

Nothing is more important than to set aside a certain period each day for writing. Once you get the habit firmly established, when that time comes you will want to write—just as when mealtime comes you want to eat. How long that writing time will be depends on you and the circumstances of your life. If you can squeeze in no more than an hour a day, set that hour aside and be true to it.

This will at first entail a certain amount of unpleasantness. Unless you have an unusually understanding and sympathetic family, you are going to find they simply do not consider that writing is "work." It's a nice little hobby for you to have, but how silly to give up everything else in order to do it. Until checks begin to speak impressively, the family is not going to take your desire for solitude at certain hours seriously. But if you don't get them to take it seriously, there aren't going to be any checks.

If you're an old softie who likes to be nice to people— well, go ahead and be an old softie. But don't expect to be a writer. If you want to write you have to get tough. How you work it out is up to you, depending on your family and your friends. Maybe you'll have to keep a supply of dime story bric-a-brac handy to fling at anybody who opens your door. You will have to snap at the Fuller Brush Man, alienate the affections of your relatives who want to come from California to visit you, make it clear to your friends who call you on the phone that this is your working hour and you will call them back, and otherwise make yourself thoroughly anti-social. Don't worry about losing all your friends. They'll be miffed for a while, but they'll come back. And when you start appearing in print they'll tell *their* friends about how they knew you when.

If you are a man your problem is simpler because you will be in a better position to retire into solitude and stay there for the required length of time. A woman's lot is harder if she has a family. You cannot completely bar your door to inter-ruptions. You will not be able to command absolute quiet while you write. But you can learn to write with wild Indians screaming under your window, and you'll find you can dis-tinguish the kind of shriek that means somebody is being killed, from the mere everyday, having-a-good-time kind of shriek. And nothing less than mayhem and murder will take you away from your typewriter. However, you may as well resign yourself to being completely unpopular with your neighbors. If you write in the morning you will have to make it clear that you cannot permit yourself to stop to listen to a choice bit of gossip whenever someone wants to run in. Or—while all the good housewives on the block hang out their wash on Monday morning, you may not get to hang yours out till Wednesday afternoon. Which will cause a great buzzing, and the rumor will undoubtedly get around that you are a little peculiar. You have to decide if you care most about what people think, or about writing.

The length of time for which you can comfortably write is something you will have to work out for yourself. It is differ-ent for every writer. By experimentation you will discover what your average wordage output is likely to be and about how much time it will take you to set down that many words. Don't be too easy, push yourself to some extent. But don't expect too much, either, or you may learn to hate the sight of a typewriter.

I work all day long, but not at one writing job. Morning is the best period for me, though for you it may be afternoon, evening, or three a.m. I know writers whose brains don't seem to come alive till after midnight. Since I prefer to write during the morning hours—say from nine to twelve—those are the hours I preserve for the important project in hand. Other writing jobs are approached after lunch and are not as sacred to laws of non-interruption as are the morning hours.

During these three hours (sometimes more when I can manage to get to my desk a little earlier) I find that I can comfortably write eight pages—about 2,000 words, as I type. By pushing myself I can write ten pages. When I push and when I take it easy is a matter I want to talk about in an-other connection later on. But when I have a project in hand, I manage at least eight pages every day. I find it wiser to set myself to a wordage limit rather than a time limit. When you tell yourself you can stop at twelve o'clock, the imp is likely to take over gleefully. "Ah!" he cries. "Nobody says I have to write so many words, or so many pages. All I have to do is sit here till twelve o'clock." And there you are likely to sit, looking out the window, daydreaming, now and then writing a grudging half page. Twelve o'clock comes and you have a page and a half of work to show for the hours you have spent at your machine.

So it is wiser to set a wordage schedule. You say to your subconscious, "Now you look here, my lad. You are going to get 2,000 words down on paper. *If* you get them down you may knock off from this particular job at twelve o'clock. If you don't get them down, back you come to finish up after lunch. And you know how you'll be hating this story by twelve o'clock." The imp, recognizing defeat, turns to, like the soldier he can be, and you get the required number of words written.

One of the first things the *writing* writer learns is that inspiration has nothing to do with it. As someone else has pointed out, it is perspiration that counts. You do not wait until you "feel" like writing. There are cycles of productiveness, to be sure. When you are in that enviable state when words pour out with facility, by all means utilize it to its utmost. But don't rely on those periods. They come all too seldom. You write doggedly every day whether you feel like it or not. And very often, in the final reading, the words you plodded over so reluctantly turn out just as well as those you poured out with ease. But you can push yourself harder during a "creative cycle," so take advantage of them when they come.

A question often asked of a writer is whether he uses a pencil or a typewriter. When some innocent asks that question in a class, the other aspirants usually titter in a slightly superior fashion. But the question is not so simple-minded as it sounds. This is a matter worth considering. Here again, experimentation will reveal the best method for you, though conditioning, too, plays its part.

Most of us probably write our first stories in pencil, if we start fairly young. This may for a time seem the most natural method. When I decided I was going to be a professional, I switched to a typewriter. I'd had no business course in school and used the hunt-and-pick method. For a number of years my stories were written clumsily by machine. Then came a period when I was a semi-invalid for six months and was forbidden a typewriter. Whereupon I took to propping a bread board against my knees and writing in pencil. I wrote a whole book during that time. (P.S. It didn't sell.) When I was well again I kept right on using a pencil, having decided that I was more comfortable without the mechanical intricacies of a typewriter taking my attention from the story. And I wrote another book which *did* sell—all in pencil.

Then something happened to my writing. Production fell off. Sales fell off. Stories came back from my regular markets. I didn't seem to fit in any more. Now I realize that I was going through a transition: I was writing myself out of the short story field into the book field, where I believe I naturally belong. Until I was willing to accept the change and acknowledge that I was no longer a short-story writer, but a writer of books, I had to go through a grim period when I seemed to be losing my touch and was reaping as many rejections as I had done in my early years of writing. The fact that the rejections were now in the form of regretful letters from editors, afforded me little comfort. The word "No" is never accompanied by a check.

Even though I did not fully understand what was happening, I knew I had to take some serious steps. I decided that for one thing I was making myself too comfortable while I wrote. I had a big armchair I snuggled into in all sorts of positions, now holding my friend the bread board on my lap, now propping it against knees hooked over the arm of the chair. I found I got sleepy very easily and that I much preferred to daydream than to write. My subconscious imp took over and encouraged me into lazier and lazier habits.

But I had not disciplined myself for long years as a writer for nothing. One day I decided that it was back to the typewriter for me and a complete new conditioning. That is worth trying if your writing habits have grown sloppy. Change everything all around. Write in a different room, or at a different hour. Make yourself start over.

This time, however, I did not mean to submit to any hunt-and-pick handicap. I got a book of typing exercises and took two weeks off from my regular writing. During those weeks I typed exercises for as long as I could bear to sit at the machine. In two weeks I had the touch system down. The experts might shudder, but I could type without watching my fingers, so I could stop worrying about the mechanics of running a typewriter. I certainly had no great speed at first, and I'm sure I did all sorts of things which would send a teacher of typing into fits—but I learned. And you can certainly go a lot faster without tiring by using a machine. To some pencil-pushers the threat of writer's cramp is a real one, and though I have never suffered seriously on that score, there were times when I stopped a morning's session with a hand that ached badly.

I am glad now that I can write with ease either on the typewriter or with pencil. Occasionally when some scene sticks and I can't seem to get it right, I will pick up a pencil and scribble it out in longhand. Very often that clears up the difficulty. Also, it is wonderful to be at ease with a pencil when you're away from home. I can write on trains, streetcars, in automobiles, on restaurant tables. It is a very handy faculty to develop.

Before we leave this subject of writing habits, I want to say something about continuous output. I know only too well the system the beginner is likely to follow, because it used to be mine. I would spend weeks getting around to writing a story. Then, with all the proper birth-pangs I would produce my masterpiece. Every word of it was dear to me. I knew confidently and whole-heartedly that it was the darling that was going to lead me to fame, fortune and publication. I sent it off with high hopes and then sat down to wait. Oh, surely for a check this time.

Of course I couldn't possibly get my mind on another piece of work until I knew my darling's fate. The magazine to which I had mailed the story had a couple of others to read besides mine, and it took anywhere from two weeks to two months to get an answer. During this time I twiddled my thumbs and waited. (The imp was on vacation having a wonderful time and encouraging me to follow *his* inclination and do nothing.) Then, sooner or later, back my little dove came winging, accompanied by a printed slip which explained that no reflection was being cast upon the worth of my manuscript, *but.* . . . In other words, *"No."* This shock of course devastated me so completely that I couldn't write at all for at least another six weeks, during which time I licked my wounds and suffered, and knew I would never in this world have another idea for a story.

You see, I didn't know any writers. I had no one to take me by the scruff of my neck and give me a good shaking. There was no one to say, "Look here, my girl, the first thing you need to learn is the professional attitude."

What is the "professional attitude"? It's just this. The minute you have a story off your hands, abandon it. It is no longer the apple of your eye, for you have given your fickle affections to a brand new apple that you had your eye on perhaps even before you finished the last story. Off with the old and on with the new. And no vacations between stories.

If your notebook is crammed with story ideas, you ought to have several "germs" already selected for your next stories before you have this one finished. You pick them out and feed them to the imp. You say, "These aren't what you're supposed to help me on now, but be a good boy and start thinking about them so you'll have some ideas the minute I need them." If you have cracked the whip often enough, he will have learned that it is pleasanter for you both if he goes vour way quietly, and he will probably do just as you tell him.

Then—when your story is in the mail, you dust off your hands and turn *immediately* to the. idea your helper has done the most with while you weren't looking. Of course by getting another story done you are building a bulwark against the discouragement a rejection slip may bring. So what if that story doesn't sell? You send it off again and you have another story to send out, too. In fact, the first thing you know you may have ten stories going the rounds all at one time, and that is a wonderful feeling. When one comes back, there are still nine other chances that you may get a check, and new ones are being added to the lot all the time.

If you want to be a professional writer *quickly,* that is the way to do it. You will not only be getting in the necessary practice to make you perfect, but you will also be getting yourself known among the editors as a producing writer. And editors are not interested in any other kind. They would rather have on call the writer who can repeat with a modest, but workmanlike job several times a year, than the brilliant once-in-five years variety. Reader following is important.

One of the things which makes me want to throw a Donald

Duck squawking spell is the writer who says, "Oh, I had a very nice letter from the editor of such-and-such, but somehow I never got around to sending in another story." In case you haven't heard, editors are busy people. They don't have any time either. They certainly don't have time to waste writing to people who take a pat on the back complacently for granted and do nothing about it. One of the reasons there are more rejection slips sent out than letters is because editors have learned to their sorrow that encouragement does not necessarily bring in more and better stories.

If an editor takes the time to send you a personal word, no matter how brief, it means that you are being noticed. It means that out of the hundreds of stories pouring over his desk, something in your story stood out sufficiently to appeal to him and make him want to see more. If you let six months go by before you send him another story, you don't deserve to sell it. When you get one of those precious letters, read that editor's magazine more carefully than ever. Slant your stories in his direction. Show him you really meant it, even if he sends the next ten stories back to you. Keep after him until he begins to feel guilty about rejecting still another story of yours. And sooner or later you'll do one that so nearly clicks that he'll be willing to tell you what's the matter with it and give you a chance to do it over. When he buys it, he'll feel an editorial pride in having discovered you.

Of course if you are to achieve this professional attitude toward your work, if you are to reach the place where your output is to be continuous, so that you turn out story after story, with no wasted time in between, then you must have a source of endless material to draw from for ideas. That is a subject for a whole chapter in itself, and first there is something else we must talk about.

V

Technique Is a Tool

This is where we get down to the serious question of how-to-do-it. The writing of fiction is not an exact science. Each writer must discover for himself his own best method of working. This he does through much experimentation.

Nevertheless, there *are* rules. Certain methods of technique have proved successful so many times that their use has been accepted by competent writers. A great many published stories disregard one or more of these rules, but that does not mean that it would be wise for you to disregard them in the beginning. Successful writers who are good craftsmen sometimes depart from the rules with a special objective in mind and to achieve some special effect. But you cannot know how a rule may be safely broken until you thoroughly understand the working of that rule.

Don't rely on intuitively and instinctively doing the right thing. *First learn the rules.* Then if you later choose to break them you can do it with purpose, not in a haphazard manner that weakens the effect of your story.

But before we consider just what these rules are, it might be as well to look at some of the difficulties likely to beset the writer who is learning about technique for the first time. Perhaps you are a person who enjoys writing. When you start a story, you just sit down and write. You haven't worried about technique, or rules, or any such irksome matters. True, your stories haven't been selling, and you would like to remedy that. So you find a critic, take a correspondence course, enroll in a class, or read a book. You are open-minded —you really do want to learn. You pick up this tool called "technique" and start using it.

The first result is apt to be alarming. You may find that for a time you lose the fluency that was yours before you started learning the rules. You find that instead of showing immediate improvement, your writing has now become stiff and self-conscious. Whatever virtue may have existed in your work vanishes and you feel that you have gone backwards and are much worse off than you were before.

This is where many novices give up. Somehow this trick of writing stories looks so much easier than it proves to be. "My goodness!" they say. "This is *work*." That it is work is something any writing writer knows full well, but that knowledge often comes as a surprise to the fellow who was merely looking over the fence.

However, if you really want to write (which may be something altogether different from wanting *to be a writer*), don't let this first awkwardness that is the natural result of learning to handle an unfamiliar tool frighten you off. Acquiring a skill is never simple. From learning to crochet to learning to drive a car, awkwardness comes first, only to give way in the end to skill, *if you persist*. If you stay with it, the rules will become so much a part of you that you can obey them without thinking about them, and the old feeling of fluency will return.

For the writer, technique is a tool with a many-faceted cutting edge. You cannot carve away with one blade and forget about the others. While you are concentrating on characterization, the movement of your story may be slowed. While you labor over your setting, characterization and plot may be out the window. Somehow you must learn to handle that many-edged tool so that everything is under control at once. This is difficult, but with practice it can be done. I know it is useless for me to warn you not to hope to sell what you write during this learning stage. No writer, including myself, can sit down at his desk without the dream of publication in his heart, without thinking surely this story must be *the* one.

But no matter how many times your dream comes to nothing, keep on with the practicing, consciously applying the many edges of your tool to the work in hand. The skill will come.

Can everyone acquire that skill? The skill of writing successful fiction? Of course not. First of all there must be native talent. This should be obvious, but it is surprising how many people set out to become writers with no natural talent at all. Probably because we all are taught from an early age to put words on paper, we are apt to think that is all there is to it. After all, the magazine we picked up last night wasn't so much. Yet that writer got paid for it. So why shouldn't we be paid, too, when we could undoubtedly do better? So our thoughts run.

How do you know whether you have any native talent as a writer? The answer to that question isn't always as easy as it might appear. Of course there are born writers—people who know from the beginning that they *must* write. That simplifies matters a lot. If you're that sort of person you are eventually going to learn and nothing is going to stop you.

You may do all the wrong things first, but despite all the fumbling and blundering and getting off on wrong feet, you'll get there.

However, many people with writing talent don't discover it until they have tried a number of other things first. Fortunately, there is no time when it is too late to start to write. You will find successful first books appearing when their authors are thirty-five, or fifty, or even sixty, and have never attempted fiction before in their lives.

I will never forget a talk I had one evening with a man who had published his first novel at sixty-five. He told me regretfully that he knew he would never now have time to say all the things he wanted to say on paper, but that he was happy he had started to write "in time."

Perhaps it is easier for a person of some maturity to begin at the beginning and learn to write than it is for the writer who is still in his twenties. One of the great handicaps of youth is the dearth of anything significant to say. Until you have lived a while, listened and learned, how can you in turn be worth listening to? So age, if anything, is an advantage.

Still, we have not answered that question concerning how you are to know whether or not you have any natural talent for writing. I think it is quite possible that the question cannot be satisfactorily answered. I think it is quite possibly a dangerous question. Certainly we cannot always judge our own work objectively and fairly. But neither is it always safe to listen to even the most competent critic on this score. Not if he tells you to stop writing. If your work is badly done and full of flaws, it may only mean that at that period in your career you have not learned enough about the rules. If I had listened to some of the people who advised me in the beginning against going ahead with what I wanted to do, I would probably never have sold a story.

Perhaps that is really the way you tell. Whatever the age at which you may begin writing, if you refuse to *stay* discouraged, if you retain your ability to bounce back every time you are laid low, if you always find yourself wanting to make one more try—then you are probably going to keep on writing until you succeed. Those who are caught by the glitter and glamour of Being an Author are not able to take it as well and the drudgery which results in only mediocre efforts will eventually discourage them into giving up.

If you are one of that group which has the writing spark, however early or late it may come to life, are there ways by which your road may be shortened? To that question I can answer with a heartfelt, "There are!" And I only wish I'd known it sooner.

True, I mailed out my first story to an editor when I was twenty-one. A very young twenty-one, with nothing of any consequence to say. It was probably necessary that I put a few years behind me just as a matter of seasoning. But even at that, my painful apprenticeship could have been shortened if I had known anything about the short-cuts.

Don't try to start at the top. That is never the way to climb a hill. All my first stories (dozens and dozens of them) were aimed at *Cosmopolitan, Saturday Evening Post, Colliers,* et al. The rejections which poured in saddened, but did not daunt me. I was going to be a writer or else. So I hurled myself at the mountain tops, picked myself up bruises and all, and tried again. This was a very wearing and silly process, and even I got tired of it after a while. Then I took my eyes off the heights long enough to observe that there were other markets at hand, less giddy and glamorous, perhaps, but also possibly more within my modest reach. I discovered the newspapers, the pulp paper magazines, the church-school publications, and after a still further apprenticeship which did not take as many years I began to sell regularly to all three.

To try for markets within reach of your capabilities is Recommendation One, and it depends entirely on you. The next recommendation draws in the outside world. If you don't know any other writers, find some. If there isn't a writers' club in your community (this is practically unbelievable), start one. If you can find no more than two other people with the itch to write (this is also fantastic), start with the three of you meeting each week. Read your manuscripts to one another and tear them apart. No pink tea party "isn't it darling!" stuff. Straight-from-the-shoulder criticism, no matter how much it hurts. The criticism may not be too good at first, if yours is a beginning group, but it will help. The purpose of these meetings is mainly to stir you into writing. Competition adds zest. If somebody over on the next block can write a story in no less than a whole month, you ought to be able to do at least as well.

I have heard a lot of harsh and scornful things said about writers' clubs, so I am eager to take this opportunity to speak up for them. "What a waste of time," say the critics. "The way to learn to write is to get busy and start writing. You don't find the real writers going to manuscript-reading fests—they're too busy."

It is true that when you begin selling your work regularly you will probably be too busy to attend meetings of this sort. It is also true that many of the "writers" found in these groups are merely hangers-on. It is always nice to say, "I belong to the Pen Pushers, you know." There are the people who want to *be* writers, rather than to write, and there is no getting away from the fact that they clutter up most writers' groups.

It is also true, however, that the beginner needs the stimulation shop talk with other writers can give him. Your professional can afford to be scornful about this because his own regular appearance in print affords him all the stimulation he needs. The beginner does not have this consolation. And what good is learning all about technique if you are not spurred to the effort of production that will make you use it.

I knew no other writers in the beginning. I made my first sales without ever exchanging a word with anyone who was bitten by the same bug which I had caught when I was very young. It was about the nicest thing that ever happened when I found that a new writers' group was starting up in Chicago and that I could join it.

The rapidity with which my nose was applied to the grindstone and kept there, was proof of how much I needed stimulation of just that type. There was nothing so thrilling as to be able to get up in a meeting and be applauded because I had just sold a story for a quarter of a cent a word, instead of being regarded with the well-so-what attitude of those who didn't understand that it wasn't the size of the check that mattered most.

After a time, as the group grew larger, we began to have professional writers come in to talk to us, and I learned to my astonishment that one didn't necessarily just sit down and write in a hit-or-miss manner. There were actually rules;

there were better ways than the haphazard methods I was using. I began for the first time to learn about the possible short-cuts I had overlooked all those years.

Somehow, you *must* learn the rules. You probably cannot do it effectively alone. There are correspondence courses, there are writing classes, there are books you can read and writers' magazines to subscribe to. You may not immediately burst into print because you are taking some course, or because you have read a book. It will take time to make the things you learn so thoroughly your own that they can work for you.

If you take a course, or enroll in a writing class, make sure of one thing: can your instructor do it himself? This is not one of those cases where it is safe to rely on the old saying about "he who can, does; he who can't, teaches." There are certain individuals whose experience in editing has perhaps given them such a well-grounded understanding of the field that they can teach without actually publishing their own material. But for the most part it pays to be suspicious. Too many teachers of writing are no more than genteel racketeers, and they are likely to do you more harm than good.

If you really mean to write, learn as much as you can about craftsmanship. Meet people with whom you can compare notes and talk shop. But don't make the mistake of turning your whole life into a schoolroom. In the final reckoning the writer is a lone wolf and too much hobnobbing with other writers will not make you a writer. That is something that lies between you and your typewriter.

Suppose at this point we have a look at the rules which govern the writing of a good story. Phases of these rules will be taken up in detail in later chapters, but we need now to take a quick glance at the many edges of this tool called "technique." Some of these rules will apply to any type of writing, but in this case we are interested mainly in applying them to the writing of juvenile fiction.

The following is a check list of questions which you may ask yourself while your story is in the making, and again when it is completed. Answers to all these questions should be in the affirmative. If any negatives show up on your question chart, that is the part of your story which needs further attention.

1. Have you a plot, a story plan?

a. Is your main character faced by a problem which it is very important for him to solve?

b. Is it a suitable problem for a child of his age?

c. Is it a problem which will interest other children? (If it is something more likely to interest and please an adult, then it is no good for your purpose.)

d. Are there real obstacles in the path of your main character which prevent him from easily achieving his purpose or goal?

e. Does he solve the problem satisfactorily at the end of the story?

2. Is your characterization sound? Are your characters real children whom the reader can see and know as individuals? Is the characterization consistent all the way through the story?

3. Does your story have significance? That is, do you have something to say that is important for young people to hear?

4. Are the various story parts satisfactorily handled?

a. Does the opening grip the interest immediately?

b. Does the action in the body of the story continue to be of absorbing interest to the age reader you are trying to reach?

c. Does the climax carry a real dramatic punch?

d. Does the denouement satisfy? No bad tastes are wanted in young people's stories. Unpleasant reality may often be presented, but the final conclusion must point constructively toward hope and leave a happy feeling.

5. Have you kept to a single viewpoint throughout the story? Does not only the speech idiom, but the thought idiom of your viewpoint character ring true all the way through the story?

6. Is your logic sound from first to last? If you strain credulity for the sake of the point you want to make, your story will fail. Just because you, the author, want something to be so, doesn't necessarily mean that it logically is so.

7. Is your dialogue natural?

8. Have you included only such material as is absolutely relevant and necessary to your plot development? Does all action, dialogue, characterization, description, help to move the story toward the climax?

9. Have you avoided the use of trite, hackneyed situations and phrases? Have you avoided the use of clichés?

10. Are your transitions quick and smooth?

11. If you have used flashbacks, are they absolutely necessary? If necessary, are they clearly handled so that your young reader is not confused and understands whether he is following past or present action?

12. Are your figures of speech those suitable to the age of the child for whom you are writing? Are they congruous?

If they make him react with "how silly!" he is going to be jarred out of the story illusion.

13. Does the story have emotional value? Does it make your reader feel? (If it doesn't, he might just as well go work a puzzle. The business of a story is to convey an emotional experience.)

14. Does the story carry the illusion of reality which makes it really seem to be happening, makes it convincing?

If you can check your story with a "yes" in answer to every one of these questions, the chances are you have a story which will sell.

VI

Perpetual Motion: Getting Story Ideas

This is the part of writing which can be the most fun. The writer trained to habits of observation never lacks for a wealth of material to write about. A good part of the time he observes and takes mental photographs of what he sees without even thinking about it. The habit has become as natural as breathing.

The beginner, on the other hand, must observe *consciously*. He must look and listen and wonder how everything that comes his way might be used in a story. Until the habit becomes second nature to him he is likely to miss three-quarters of the story ideas which are teeming all around him. The writer who envies other writers their eye for detail has only to get busy and consciously develop that sort of eye in himself.

He must launch himself on various idea-collecting projects. He must start files and notebooks and work out various systems for waking himself up to the point where he can recognize a story idea the second it raises its head. All this is fun. It is a sort of game, more play than work. Maybe he has a file of pink cards for characters, blue cards for plots, etc. He sees a small girl he'd like to use in a story and he rushes home to jot his data down in the proper section of his file. He has folders for newspaper and magazine clippings, all rich with story ideas, and every day he marks the newspaper dutifully, clips his selections, files them under such headings as "Story Germs," "Hobbies," "Settings," and the rest, all the way down the line. He may even work out a cross-filing system whereby he can find any given item at a moment's notice.

This is all very fine and can be extremely profitable. But do it with one eye on that imp. Because he is going to love it. This is no work for him at all and he'll start whispering in your ear, "Isn't this fascinating? Aren't we working hard? Look how professional we're being! All these wonderful things to write about!" And because he kids you into thinking you're being a writer, you may find yourself spending all your time collecting material and *getting ready* to write, instead of actually sitting down and writing (which is the last thing in the world your subconscious wants you to do).

You will certainly need to keep notebooks of ideas, but don't let your system, whatever it is, get too elaborate. Don't forget that the time you spend clipping and filing might very well be better spent at the typewriter *writing*.

The lower drawer in my cabinet always fascinates young writers. It is packed with clippings and pictures of all kinds, neatly arranged under various headings. I keep it as a sort of Exhibit A, but the last date on those clippings runs back over ten years ago. Fortunately I got too busy writing my ideas into stories to spend time on that file.

At present my "filing" system is pared to the bone. I have a folder headed "Current Work" into which I put various odds and ends pertaining to jobs on hand at the moment. This folder is kept so busy that it sits constantly on my desk and is never put away in the cabinet.

When I am working on a book of fiction I keep a large looseleaf notebook into which goes all the preparatory material concerning the book. This is likely to be too unwieldy to be kept in a folder.

I also keep on hand a smaller notebook which can be tucked into my purse and carried about with me, or if I am at home, can be kept near by whatever I may be doing. Into this goes (in not too tidy fashion) ideas concerning any of my various jobs. Quite often when I am reviewing someone else's book, an apparently unrelated idea will pop into my mind concerning my own book. This I will want to jot down quickly before it is lost. These ideas can come anywhere, whether I am riding on a train, waiting in a dentist's office, or shopping for groceries. If I tell myself to write it down later, I know I'll probably forget—hence the ever-present notebook.

The rest of my "system" consists of a couple of big brown envelopes into which go records, clippings, notes, any data at all which may concern the book after next, and the book after that. It would be more workmanlike to put this material into neatly labeled folders in my file, but somehow I never seem to get around to labeling the folders.

Since I no longer write short stories I have dispensed with the desultory note-taking in which the short story writer must indulge. Since each of my projects takes a number of months to complete, I make my notes and collect material with a definite purpose in mind, and as little waste motion as possible.

But if you are just breaking in, I hope you mean to write short stories first. Even if you find, as I did, that you are better suited by temperament to the writing of books, I suggest that you spend a thorough apprenticeship in the short story field, before you attempt a book. Working with the shorter length will condition you so thoroughly to telling a story and keeping it moving, that when you start to write books you will not be able to shake off that habit. When I pick up a book for young people and find it slow and rambling, lacking in pace, not getting anywhere fast enough, I know the writer has not had this much-needed training in the short story field. It is much easier to write a book than it is to write a short story. Therefore, learn the more difficult form first and be forever after grateful for the things it will teach you.

In writing a short story for young people you learn first of all that interest must never let down at any point. Being forced to put your story into the confines of a really difficult wordage limit (say 2,000 words), you learn to free yourself of any clutter of descriptive material, or of detail unnecessary to your single purpose of making that story move ahead.

I learned that the end of the scene in a story can be a danger point and that I must, before there was any faint slowing of interest on the part of my young reader, throw in some new matter, connected directly of course with the main story problem, but raising some new issue of success or defeat. I must not fail to rouse in his mind a question which he cannot bear to let go unanswered. A story which draws a reader's interest on from scene to scene by such a method inevitably has pace. It moves and there is always something interesting happening.

Having learned this rule in writing short stories for young people, I did not need to conquer it in writing a book. It was something I continued to inject into my longer stories and as a consequence reader interest appears to stay with me from first to last chapter, and there is no danger (whatever other faults they may have) of my books being put aside in boredom because the writer "doesn't get to the story." It is amazing how long some book writers take to get to their stories and I cannot help but feel that if they had gone through a rigorous training period in the shorter form they would write much more interesting books.

My own eventually pared-down system of note-taking when I was writing short stories consisted of keeping four notebooks. Two of them were medium-sized looseleaf notebooks, one the usual hard-working purse size, and, fourth, a small looseleaf book. One of the middle-sized books was kept faithfully as a plot book, and was one of my most important sources of story ideas. The second took a lot of time to keep up, but I am glad I was able to keep it for a number of years because it is still useful to me in many ways. I read always with a pencil in hand and when I came across a passage in some book or story which struck me as unusually significant, I would copy it into my notebook. In it are paragraphs from the books of Thomas Mann, Somerset Maugham, Rebecca West, and a great many others. In it, too, are pertinent passages from the autobiographies of various writers—Arnold Bennett, Edna Ferber, Gamaliel Bradford. Included as well are sections from various books on psychology.

This has become for me a stimulating book to pick up and glance through at any time—a sort of personal "Elbert Hubbard" of my own. I frequently regret that I can no longer take time to add to that collection.

The use of the purse-size book I have already mentioned.

Into it will go anything at all that appeals to you at the very time when it comes to mind. Most of this can be regarded as plot-germ material and later typed into the plot book.

The fourth book is an alphabetical listing of names. First names and last names, foreign names, names for boys and girls. To make a collection of that kind is simple enough, takes practically no time, and can save you much thinking and searching when you want to name a character. You can start such a book simply by jotting down all the names you can think of. After that you collect names from every book or story you read, or any unusual name you may hear.

So much for what you do with your ideas, once you have them. Now for that well-worn question: "Where do you get your ideas?"

Everywhere, of course, is the answer, but let's be a bit more specific than that. Once you have that "seeing eye" developed you'll collect ideas constantly. By way of an experiment, the next time you go downtown and walk through a department store, try waking yourself up just before you leave the store. You've been intent on your purchases probably, but now suppose you retrace your steps looking for story material. It is amazing how the color and bustle of that store will suddenly come alive for you and be a thousand times more interesting than when you walked down that same aisle blindly a few minutes before.

The clerks behind the counters are characters now. So are the customers. The entire scene is rich with atmosphere and plot material. But remember—you're going to write for children, so you have to look at this from the angle of your young reader. What would attract a small boy on this aisle? A small girl? Or a teen-ager?

Do you really know, or are you just guessing? I can think of no better way for a writer to find out what attracts children than to take a group of youngsters of varying ages on a shopping tour and give them their heads. You may spend the next day in bed, but you'll be led in unexpected directions and you'll learn a lot.

Sensory perception is of primary importance to the young child. He reacts keenly to color and size and shape, to sound and smell, and very, very strongly to touch. Upon seeing some object he has not hitherto met in the course of experience, the first reaction of the young child is to reach out his hand to touch it. Having made its acquaintance through eager fingertips, having found whether it is smooth or rough, hot or cold, soft or hard, he is then prepared to take it into the ever-expanding boundaries of his world and give it a recognizable place. It is this desire to touch which has given rise to such popular little numbers as *Pat the Bunny,* and other books in which actual materials are used to give the small child the experience of touching various surfaces and textures.

But these devices are mere stunts. The writer has at his disposal the use of figures of speech which will link the new to the already known and so is not bound to the field of touch alone. What is more, a writer who is wise enough to use sensory perception to the fullest degree in his stories, will bring to the scenes he describes that illusion of reality without which any story falls flat.

One of the most useful purposes to be served by books for children is to introduce the young reader to new experiences that he might not meet in the course of everyday living and thus broaden his horizons in many directions. This can be achieved in great part by learning to know the sensory details which attract children of different ages and using them fully in one's writing.

At any rate, stir up your imagination and see what you get. It may be a little sluggish and slow to respond at first, but if you keep prodding, it will get the idea and be constantly at work.

Wherever you go, collect sounds and odors and the feel of things. Even the taste. And I don't mean only the taste of food. Dry, dusty air has a taste. So has fresh, salty sea air, or sunny country air, or air heavy with fog. In touching objects, think about how they feel. Are they warm to the fingers or cold? Are they limp-feeling, or hard, rough or smooth? What other familiar objects do these things resemble? Don't rely only on your fingers for touch sensation. How does snow feel against your face? Or water against your body? How does that inviting pillow feel behind your back?

If you make the habit of collecting details of this kind wherever you go, you will find your writing enriched and enlivened far beyond the cost of the slight trouble it will take to develop the habit of using all your senses as a writer. Children, especially, are lovers of detail, and they will prize your stories if you can bring alive in words their own everyday world, as well as some new world to which your story introduces them.

Of course your main source of idea material will be your own past experiences. "Write about what you know" is advice given so often to young writers that they are apt to run from hearing it one more time. For some curious reason the young writer seldom wants to write about what he knows. Not having as yet developed that "seeing eye" which recognizes story material everywhere, he feels that only the things he knows nothing whatsoever about are interesting. I went through this foolish state—I know what it's like.

I spent the first fifteen years of my life in the Orient. I had the most vivid memories of China and Japan and the Philippine Islands. But while other young writers I knew were trying to sell stories about a Shanghai they had never seen, I was bent on writing about Hollywood night clubs— which I had never seen. To me the Orient was everyday stuff and not half so exciting as America. When I got out of school I worked for several years selling books in department stores. Nothing seemed more tiresome to me and I went home at night to spend my writing hour describing the lives of people I knew nothing about.

One of the quickest ways to start selling is to recognize the rich ore which exists right in your own back yard, however prosaic it may look to you. After a while I woke up and began to write stories of American children in the Orient for the church-school papers, and of course they sold because I knew what I was talking about. Years later, when I was no longer selling books, I began to see the glamorous and fascinating aspects of book-selling, and wrote *A Star for Ginny*, which is about a girl working at her first job in the book section of a department store. In fact, my time in a department store netted me three books laid against that background.

In time, however, you may reach the stage when you have exhausted that back-yard material. You may go into a discouraging slump when all is dust in your mouth and you feel completely dried up when it comes to story ideas. Your notebooks and files net you nothing but yawns and you suffer the quite painful frustration of a writer who wants to write, but has nothing to say. This is serious and it is likely to come at one time or another to every writer. Sometimes this only means that you are in a transition period and are now ready for the next step up. You may be writing yourself out of your old markets and yet be unwilling to relinquish them completely before you are sure of yourself in a new field. Or it may mean that you really have used up the stock of material in your memory storehouse and have neglected to fill those empty shelves with fresh goods.

In either case the treatment is not to sit around at home slumped on the back of your neck, while you wait for a story idea to come in and bite you. The thing to do at that point is to go out and bite a few story ideas.

I came out of my worst slump with a rule which has been so useful to me that I have never since that time run out of ideas. It is just this: *Interest follows action.* First you *do* something—then you get interested. So many people think it should be the other way around and that you have to be interested before you care about doing anything. This, of course, gets you nowhere.

Following this rule, you can pull yourself out of any slump by picking a subject out of the air. It makes not the slightest difference whether you have any interest in it or not. When you start doing something about it the interest will come and the door will open that will lead somewhere.

The first time I applied this rule, the subject I picked was "department store advertising." Probably it came to mind because at the conclusion of *A Star for Ginny* my heroine was going into the advertising department to work as an artist. As a matter of fact, I remember finishing the book with a feeling of relief because *I* knew nothing about the work she meant to enter and certainly couldn't write about it at that point.

At any rate, that was the dry-as-dust (as far as I was concerned) subject to which I decided to apply my interest-follows-action rule. Regardless of my apathy toward the subject, I would force myself out of my comfortable armchair and into the field. Bored as I was at the prospect, I would find out something about department store advertising at first hand.

The exciting thing about this sort of adventurous undertaking (and it certainly is that) is that you never know where you'll end up. The chances are you will branch off down some fascinating side road leading to undreamed-of shores. I did not write a book about department store advertising. I still know absolutely nothing about the subject, but that was my springboard. It was the thing that started me off on a quest that brought me as rich a collection of new experiences and new material to write about as I could have hoped to find.

Do you know how a sponge feels? You'd better figure it out because you need to make yourself into a sort of animated sponge when you start the action which is going to create interest in your apathetic soul. You are going to soak up everything that comes along. You are going to reject nothing. Through every pore you are going to take in material until that moment when the electric switch is thrown that will bring interest enthusiastically to life for weeks and months to come.

The first step is the hardest to take because of the weight of inertia. It is so much easier to drift along and make no effort than to stand up and push yourself into action. The first push I gave myself was toward an appointment with a girl who wrote advertising in a department store. I went up to see her, not too hopefully, but armed with a notebook.

Her office was a cubbyhole, and she was terribly busy. I was permitted to sit in a corner and wait. I waited and things began to seep in through my sponge pores, whether I invited them or not. To begin with, this wasn't the sort of office I'd ever seen before. It could have been very drab and ugly, but its pretty, smart-looking occupant had covered all the wall space from floor to ceiling with pages torn from various magazines. There were fascinating color photographs, interesting black-and-whites, stunning advertisements. I could never have dreamed up that room sitting at home twiddling my thumbs. I had to go out and expose myself to it. Even in my lackluster state I determined that if I could ever again think of a story I would have to put that office into it. Eventually the office went into not one, but two full-length books.

As I sat there waiting, things kept happening. People popped in and out, chattering about their various store problems. It was all very informal and nobody paid any attention to me. I didn't know it, but somewhere in my subconscious a hand was moving stealthily toward that electric switch.

When the girl I had come to see had time to talk to me, I told her I was planning to write a career book for girls about department store advertising and would she tell me a little about her job. The wonderful part about approaching story ideas in this manner is that you never know what is around the next corner, or how suddenly you may be plunged into an Alice-in-Wonderland world.

My chosen "career-girl" began to talk obligingly enough about her job, and I found that she didn't write the sort of advertising I'd had vaguely in mind. She wrote copy for all the sign cards that were used throughout the store and in the show windows. Writing sign copy, it seemed, was quite an art. You not only wrote it, you designed the card itself in some cases, indicating the materials which would make it up, and the colors which were to be used. The colors, of course, had to fit in with the display to be shown in the window.

"You ought to see our window display department," she said. "I should think that would be an awfully interesting place for a writer."

The hand reached the switch and on went a blinding light where there had been only darkness for months past. I'd jumped off the springboard and was on my way swimming for an unknown shore. It was all settled in an instant. I was going to write a vocational novel for girls about window decorating, and I knew without a doubt that I was going to have the time of my life finding out all about the subject. What was more, I was going to expose myself to the biggest rash of story ideas any writer ever caught.

It wasn't always easy. I had to pull more than one string, and be very persistent before I wangled my way back of the scenes into a window display department. Very little had been written on the subject and I found I had to get nearly all my material firsthand. The assistant display manager at one store took an interest in what I wanted to do and let me trail around after him, notebook in hand, taking down everything I saw and heard, asking foolish questions, soaking up atmosphere.

He was particularly interested in showing me one big

room in the department which was lined all the way around with cabinets. In these cabinets were arms, legs, heads, torsos and all the various parts of window mannequins. Another light clicked on and I thought, "Mm, what a wonderful place for a murder." By the time I went home that day I knew that I was still going to write a book for girls about window decorating, but before I did that I was going to write a murder mystery for adults against exactly the same background.

Out of that experience, out of going out and exposing myself to story ideas, came the two books: *Red Is for Murder* and *A Window for Julie*. By the time I finished them I could practically qualify as a window decorator myself. It was work—I had to spend hours on the scene; collecting material. I stood outside many a window display writing down things I had never noticed before in my casual shopping tours. But out of reality came story material in richly rewarding quantities. One of the notes I made had to do with a large spray gun I noticed among the odds and ends of the display department. I asked if they were bothered with flies and was told that gun contained a pine concoction which had been sprayed around the store at Christmas time. I had no idea what I could do with a pine spray, but I wrote it down in my notebook. Later it helped to solve my mystery story. A pair of fascinating pink horses used in a baby window display so intrigued me that I worked them into the climax of my girls' book.

I have told about this experience in detail because I feel that this system is one of the best you can possibly use to stimulate the imagination and get yourself launched on more story ideas than you can write in a lifetime. It is a lot of trouble, but never too much trouble. Such material, once stored away in notebooks and memory, can serve you end-lessly from that time on. Nothing is ever wasted.

One of the special virtues of getting story material in this fashion is the fact that it is likely to give your story that "different" touch which may appeal to an editor. Editorial desks are swamped with stories about the same old stuff. Old stuff is good if handled in a fresh new way, or if some of the story elements are so outstanding that they make the story irresistible. But if you are just breaking in and want to at-tract attention, the quickest way to do it is by getting some-thing novel and unusual into your story.

One of the requests I hear most often from teen-age girls is, "Give us stories about *us*. Give us stories about things that are happening to us *now*." In writing *A Window for Julie* I was writing about the girls of today, about their boy problems and job problems, but I was also getting into the book an interesting background which is unfamiliar to most readers. If you can combine the contemporary and the unusual, you have a practically sure-fire sale. Providing, of course, you have by that time learned to handle all the other cutting edges of that tool of technique.

In this matter of going to reality for your material, I'd like to make one point. Sooner or later every critic or editor has the experience of condemning a manuscript, only to have the writer counter with the protest, "But it really happened." I hope you will never be guilty of bringing up that age-old defense. That it really happened doesn't mean a thing. Very often things which really happen are not good story material at all because they are much too coincidental and farfetched to be believed as fiction. The point is not whether something happened, but whether you can make the reader *believe* it happened. So while you are collecting your material in the field, remember that it must in the final reckoning be blended into fiction. It will have a firm grounding in reality, but it will be an interpretation of reality, rather than life itself.

VII

Three Necessary Ingredients:
EMOTION, SIGNIFICANCE, IMMEDIACY

The best definition I know of a short story is one which Frederic Nelson Litten gave to his fiction writing classes at Northwestern University: "A short story is a narrative with an emotional purpose."

Intellectual pyrotechnics on paper seldom make the sort of writing that lasts. If you look back to those stories and books you have remembered over the years you will find that in every case they gave you an *emotional experience*. Whether the emotion was one of delight, elation, pity, anger, disgust —whatever it was, in reading that story or book you were made to *feel*.

It is in this matter particularly that the beginner's manuscript falls flat. The reader, putting the story down, feels nothing at all. His major reaction is "so what?" This is far too often true of stories for children, even of some which get published. Perhaps the writers have been so long out of touch with the things about which children feel strongly that they are no longer able to capture such emotion on paper and transfer it to a reader.

But a book like Miriam Powell's *Jareb*, which is the story of a boy in Georgia's pine woods country and his love for a dog considered worthless, will never be forgotten by anyone who reads it. Because the reader feels with the emotions of the young hero, he lives the story on every page. For a different kind of emotion—laughter—*Homer Price* by Robert McCloskey is already becoming something of a modern classic. *The Hundred Dresses* by Eleanor Estes *hurts* when you read it. It hurts deep down inside so that the young reader will never forget it and never want to be like the children in the story.

The story is about a little girl named Wanda Petronski who lives in a small American town and goes to a public school. Her house is shabby, she wears queer clothes and has an awfully funny name.

One day the most popular girl in school appears in a lovely new dress. That dress catches Wanda's eye and she tells the children that she has some beautiful dresses, too. A hundred of them, all different, all lined up in her closet at home.

This remark of Wanda's starts what the children call "the dresses game." They tease and torment Wanda about her hundred dresses. Only Maddie, the child who is the viewpoint character in the story, is a little troubled by what the others are doing. But like so many well-intentioned people, she stands by and does nothing to mend the situation.

Then the school holds a dress design contest in which all the girls may enter drawings. On the day the contest ends Maddie comes to school to find her room bright with beautiful pictures hung all around the walls. Pictures of a hundred dresses, all different, painted by Wanda Petronski. Unfortunately Wanda is no longer in the school to know that she has won the contest. The teacher has a letter from Wanda's father which she reads to the class.

Mr. Petronski has decided to take his children away to

live in the big city where Petronski will not be such a funny
name, and where nobody will "holler Pollack."

Maddie feels pretty awful about this and she writes
Wanda a letter. Not to say she is sorry, because children
don't know how to apologize, but just to tell Wanda that she
has won the contest and to say how much they all like her
pictures. A long time after a letter comes back from Wanda,
written not to Maddie, but to the teacher. She says she likes
her new school and she does not want the pictures of the
hundred dresses because now she has a hundred more dresses,
all different, all lined up in her closet at home. But she wants
two special pictures to go to her friends Maddie and Peggy.

Maddie takes her picture home, puts it up on the wall of
her room and sits down to look at it. There she discovers the
secret. Wanda had drawn her—Maddie—into the picture,
and Maddie understands that through it all Wanda only
wanted to be friends.

There is no pounding home of any moral, but through the
significant happenings in the story the emotions of the reader
are reached in a way he will never forget.

In his book on *Writing Non-Fiction*, Walter S. Campbell
(Stanley Vestal) makes a point which is worth consideration
by the fiction writer:

"Men differ greatly in their thoughts, far less in their
emotions, and hardly at all in their sensations."

If you want to put across a thought (an idea, a moral) in
your story, don't begin with that. Before you can reach your
reader and make him come over to your side in his beliefs,
you must reach him through his emotions. You must make
him *feel*. In order to make him feel, let him experience a
sensation of some kind. Understanding, tolerance, are not

common to all men. If Eleanor Estes had preached about them in *The Hundred Dresses* she would have lost part of her audience. But by causing the reader to identify himself with a character in the story, hurt to that character becomes hurt to the reader. Hurt is a sensation familiar to all of us, and so we feel with and for Wanda and unconsciously take to heart the lesson her story teaches.

If you are going to touch the emotions of your reader, if you are going to make him feel deeply, if you are going to make him care about your story people, care what happens to them, you must understand first of all what your reader wants of life. And you must be warmly sympathetic toward his wants. There is a universality about human needs, no matter what the age or position of the person. When you thoroughly understand that, there will be no danger of your "writing down" and your stories will take on a warmth that will make your readers react to them with genuine feeling.

Anyone who knows the children's field will tell you that a good story for children should be enjoyed by any age at all. It should not bore the mother who is reading it aloud, even though it is the slight story contained in a picture book. *Tom Sawyer, Treasure Island, Wind in the Willows*—any book you can mention which will live through the years— can be read and enjoyed by anyone. These books have the quality of universality because the author understood *people*.

What your small boy reader wants of life is not so very different from what you want of it. He wants affection, he wants to be approved of, he wants to have a sense of his own worth in the scheme of things, he wants to feel that there are "adventures" to be met even in the course of everyday living. And so you write stories about boys just like him. You prove that there are "adventures" to be found around almost any corner. You show him how the character in the story got off on the wrong foot so that people didn't like him much, and then learned how to win approval in a very pleasant way. (Remember Charcoal?)

When you are writing for older children, your task is exactly the same. That teen-age girl who will be your reader wants other young people to like her. She wants to straighten out school problems, boy problems, job problems. She wants to feel that life doesn't have to be a dull, repetitious routine forever and forever. So in your story you help to straighten out these things, you help her over the rough spots that are sure to come, and you help her to understand the good old rule about life being what you make it. If you can't sympathize with what your readers want of life, if you cannot look upon people of all sorts and all ages with generosity and compassion, then you have no business trying to be a writer.

Significance and emotion are tied together closely. If you want your reader to feel emotion while he is reading your story, you must have something to say. Most stories which have something to say will be found to have a theme. It is a good idea to set down in a single sentence just what you want to say in your story. Sometimes when you analyze old stories you have written (the ones that didn't sell) you will find that you were trying to say at least six different things in 2,500 words. Better pick one main thread and hew to it all the way through. In a book you may have a major theme and several minor contributing themes, but in the space of a short story you had better confine yourself to one clear thought.

Here are a few themes I have used in short stories:

1. Under the superficial differences all people are the same.

2. A popular girl who is always sure of herself and runs other people's lives with a high hand may need to learn that she, too, can be mistaken.

3. A sacrifice made for another may reap the giver a rich reward.

I suggest that you start jotting your own themes down in that plot notebook. A theme is anybody's property and may be used over and over again in stories that will bear no resemblance to other stories written around the same theme. The Bible is of course filled with themes. Any book of proverbs will net you hundreds. It is a profitable idea to analyze every story you read for its underlying theme and add that theme to your collection.

If you work a theme into your story and handle it well you can be sure that story will carry significance. Editors in the children's field are always looking for writers who have something worth saying. Too, a theme will help to give your story a single effect. Without a theme your story parts may be scattered around loosely in an unconnected fashion, like beads unstrung. The theme is the thread that gathers all your beads into one firm strand that begins at a set point and ends at a set point.

The third necessary ingredient in your story is immediacy. That means that you must give your reader the feeling that something is happening *now*. Blocks of information are sure interest-killers. In order to test your writing in this matter it is a good idea to regard your story as a play. Then ask yourself if the scene is being performed before your eyes, or if a narrator has stepped out in front of the curtain to talk about the play? Away with narrators! No one has time to listen to them these days. Give us action, give us something happening *right now*.

Here is an example of the wrong and the right way to handle a scene.

> Julie went up to the display department to get the stork and take it down to the window. But when she reached the department she found that the bracket which had held the stork was empty. This disturbed her very much, but she thought one of the helpers must have carried it downstairs. Finally she walked across the room and discovered with horror that the stork had fallen to the floor and been broken to bits.

In that version somebody is telling us about it; we are not watching Julie with our own eyes. Now let's raise the curtain on the play and see how it looks when the same scene was presented with immediacy in *A Window for Julie*.

> There were no lights burning in the department, and for a moment Julie thought she heard someone moving in one of the rooms.
>
> "Hello!" she called. "Who's there?"
>
> But there was no answer and the sound of her own voice echoing through emptiness had a startling effect on her nerves. Gracious, she thought, was she going to start believing in ghosts at this late date? A window display department would certainly make a wonderful place to haunt! She chuckled at her foolish thoughts and hurried to the door of the workroom. It was dark and she had to fumble a moment for the light. Her fingers found the switch, turned it, and the room sprang

into life in all its familiar aspects. But Julie stood in the doorway in startled dismay, scarcely believing the evidence of her own eyes.

The bracket which held the stork was empty.

There could be only one explanation, of course. One of the helpers had come up for it on his own, not knowing that she meant to carry it down herself. Probably it was already in the window by now and Bill was busy hanging it.

That was what she wanted to believe, but something held her there in the doorway. Then, almost as if she moved against her will, she stepped quietly into the room, walked around Kim's worktable, and stood staring in horror. What remained of her precious stork lay shattered at her feet.

The first example is mere summary. The second gives the scene in detail as it happens, and if we have followed the story up to that point we can experience the same shock of horror Julie feels.

At times when it is necessary to get over unimportant happenings in a hurry, you may need to summarize. But never summarize your important scenes—show them happening. And remember that even necessary summary is deadening to the interest, so don't clutter up your story with it.

Before we leave this matter of Julie's stork I'd like to make a further point concerning the tremendously important factor of emotion. While you can understand the advantage the second version of this scene has over the first, I am sure that you did not feel any particular emotion in reading the scene. That is because you had not read what went before. You could not know how much depended on that stork as far as Julie was concerned. Emotion is something which is built up in a story from the first paragraph. It is built up through liking and sympathy for the character, through understanding of the problem which faces her and a grasping of how much depends on her success.

In this case, if the window Julie has planned is not ready by the following morning (and it is already evening) she will lose her job; a rival she detests will succeed in her place, she will have failed in her own estimation, and she will have missed proving to the boy she is in love with that she can make good, thus losing his respect. She will also be a discredit to the older woman who has befriended her and taught her about window decorating.

Because of all these things the girl reader is as dismayed as Julie at this point. In order to make the most of the emotion we have aroused in the reader and in order to make the contrasting relief and satisfaction we want her to feel at the end of the story as keen as possible, we must be sure that things go from bad to worse, building up the sort of suspense which will not permit the reader to lay the book down at this point. One of the men who is working in the window tells Julie they'll have to go ahead without the stork and while the window will be ordinary, it won't be too bad.

If I let the story follow those lines the letdown in reader interest would be immediate. So I point up the fact that an "ordinary" window means failure as far as Julie is concerned. And I make things as tough as possible.

It is too late to buy a new stork—all the stores are closed. The stork cannot be mended. Julie has only till morning to work this out. She hasn't the faintest idea what to do. (At this point in the plotting there was a time when the author also hadn't the faintest idea what to do.)

Then the hero comes upon the scene and tells her this is no time to quit. They are going for a walk to get ideas. He takes her down South Wabash where there are a lot of junk shops. They are all closed and not a stork is to be seen in any window.

At this point, if the author had not put in a lot of field work before she wrote the book, she, like Julie, might have been stumped for good. But paging through my notebook, looking for an inspiration, I came across a reference to two wooden horses I had seen in a window. They were lovely pink horses with flowing gold manes and they had so caught my eye that I had asked the display man about them. He told me that originally they had been an unpleasant purple color, and I had dutifully written this down in my notebook.

The horses were just what I needed. So there they were for Julie to find in one of the windows of a closed shop. Not pink, but a dreadful purple. I did not permit my hero to recognize the worth of those horses, because if I had, he would have solved Julie's problem. *Always remember that your leading character must solve the story problem through her own doing.* So of course it is Julie who visualizes those purple horses as they may be used to save her window. She refuses to listen to Kim's objection that storks, not horses, bring babies, and that she cannot possibly use anything purple in her pink and blue baby window. What Julie means to do with those horses is held out on the reader (by having Julie hold out on Kim) and further suspense is built up until the very moment when the window is uncovered and a thoroughly satisfying *emotion* is aroused in the reader.

Make your reader feel. Have something to say. Show it happening now.

VIII

THE CHICKEN OR THE EGG:
I. THE CHICKEN, CHARACTERIZATION

I have known writers to carry on endless controversies concerning the primary importance of (a) characterization, (b) plot. One school claims that the plot is of no consequence and will grow naturally enough out of character action, once you get your characters worked out so they can take over. *Character* is All Important. The second school claims that plot is of first importance, and until you know what sort of story you are going to tell you can't even know what type of characters you'll need to use. *Plot* is All Important.

When the argument becomes sufficiently heated and the two groups start calling names, the first uses the scornful term "commercial" toward the second, and the second comes right back with scathing remarks about "art-for-art's sake." And nobody gets anywhere.

In my own modest opinion (and I realize that both groups will probably jump on me) plot and characterization are inextricably wound together. To discuss which comes first is as futile as to argue the old chicken-or-the-egg controversy. I am taking the chicken first, not because I consider it of primary importance—I don't; I consider it of *equal* importance—but because I have to start somewhere.

If you are having difficulty in the matter of getting emotion into your stories, it may be that some of the trouble lies in poor characterization. Of course, without understanding, sympathy, insight into a child's nature, no writer for children can get very far. But starting from that basis of understanding, the next requirement is a knowledge of the tools by which you characterize. Having learned what they are, you will next learn to use them by consistent practice. Finally you will need a measuring stick to test each story when it is completed.

Long before you reach the point of putting words on paper you decide certain things about your fictional children. You choose first of all a viewpoint character. If you are writing for children, do, please, make your viewpoint character a child. It is amazing how often writers who are starting out in this field will pick an adult for a viewpoint character. Someone whose problems and interests are not a child's problems and interests. Your young reader wants to see your story through young eyes like his own. If you happen to be writing an animal story in which you cannot write from the viewpoint of a child, then see that your main character is a young animal. I cannot plead too often with the writer of children's stories to use children for characters and keep adults to a role of minimum necessity. There are already too many interfering grownups in the life of any young person.

A successful exception to this rule is Helen Earle Gilbert's delightful *Mr. Plum and the Little Green Tree,* published a number of years ago. Mr. Plum is an old shoemaker and the only other character of importance in the story is the Mayor. There are no children in the book at all.

Perhaps the author succeeds because quite old people have rather childlike qualities. And Mr. Plum's problem in the story is one with which small children will sympathize. There is a little green tree in the little green square across from Mr. Plum's shop. The tree is about to be cut down by men sent out by the Mayor. Mr. Plum takes it upon himself to save the tree and the story is about how he succeeds.

The book is worth studying for the excellent characterization of Mr. Plum, for the plot, and for the emotional tug the story carries. None of these ingredients is to be found too often in picture books. Applying to this story Mr. Campbell's statement about people differing greatly in their thoughts, less in their emotions, and hardly any at all in their sensations, we find that the author has achieved her effect by using that process. That a tree should not be cut down is a thought. It will have no effect as such upon the child who is reading the book unless he is reached first through sensation and emotion. Any child may behold and delight in the beauty of a tree, as Mr. Plum delights in this tree. That is a sensation common to everyone. From there he may be led to love the tree, as Mr. Plum loves this tree. Love is an emotion. Once feeling has been aroused in the reader, the cutting down of the tree becomes a major calamity, rather than a remote thought to which no emotional tags are attached.

Nevertheless, despite Mr. Plum, it is wiser in the beginning not to make your main characters adults. Don't attempt it at all in the short story form, since most editors will not be interested. If you have such a character up your sleeve, it is better to use him only in a picture book for younger children. The older the child, the less likely it is that he will be interested in an adult character in the main role.

If you want your story to carry an emotional impact it is wise to select one character and tell the story from his viewpoint clear through. Otherwise you will be jumping around from the emotional outlook of one child to another and there will be an effect of confusion for the reader. If you write from a single viewpoint you will present nothing that character cannot see and hear and feel and smell. You will present no thoughts which are not his thoughts, unless they are given through the spoken words of others and he is on the spot to hear them. No matter how exciting a scene may be going on in the next room, unless you can devise a logical means for getting Johnny into that room, don't try to present that scene in your story.

So many writers break this elementary rule that it cannot be emphasized too often. If your viewpoint skips from character to character throughout the story, you scatter your shots, weaken the emotional effect. And every time you switch viewpoints you cause an inevitable letdown in story interest.

Not only are beginners the offenders in this matter of viewpoint. Book after published book comes my way in which it is obvious that the writer has never heard of the rule of single viewpoint, and what is worse, the editor has let him get away with it. Some people call it the "omniscient" viewpoint, but that term lends the practice a dignity to which I refuse to subscribe. Rarely indeed does this vague, all-over-the-place viewpoint help a story.

Way back in the beginning I said that there were no absolute rules for writing. The advice to write from a single viewpoint is as close to being an absolute rule as any a teacher may give you. At least train yourself in the habit until you can fully appreciate its advantages. Once having done that, you may never want to write any other way. Or if you do decide later to break the rule, you will know why you are doing so and how to do it. You will not be falling sloppily into a bad habit because you don't know any better.

In a full-length book, viewpoint may be changed to various characters if you retain the single viewpoint throughout the course of each chapter. *Don't* shift viewpoint several times in one chapter, and above all don't shift it several times on one page. If you are writing a short story you'll do a much more workmanlike job if you retain the single viewpoint straight through the story.

The first person story is, of course, the perfect example of single viewpoint writing. It is very easy to hold to one viewpoint when the leading character is "I." But first person writing is not very popular with young readers and is therefore frowned upon by editors except in some especially good stories. Every librarian has had the experience of hearing some child say, "But I don't like 'I' books!"

It is more difficult to retain the single viewpoint when you are writing in the third person. If you have difficulty in getting the hang of it at first, it is good practice to write in the first person just to get the feeling of it. Then you can change the story into third person after it is written. You'd better recognize the prejudice which exists against first person stories in the children's field and not try to sell the story in that form.

If you are uncertain concerning which of your characters to choose for point of view, select the one to whom the most trouble is likely to happen. Conflict, trouble, disaster, all mean story interest, and it is much better to tell the story from Johnny's viewpoint if he is likely to be faced by serious difficulties, than it is to use sister Sue's, if she is more likely to be a disinterested onlooker.

At any rate you must identify yourself thoroughly with your viewpoint character. You must not only keep to the idiom of speech he would use in speaking, but you must also keep to the idiom of his thought, which is most difficult of all.

If you are writing from the viewpoint of a child who is watching his mother across the room, don't have him think: "Mother seemed preoccupied that evening." "Preoccupied" is a natural enough word for you to use, but it is not in the idiom of the child about whom you are writing and if you are to stay in the shoes, in the skin, in the mind of that child, you will be more likely to have him think: "Mother seemed awfully quiet that evening." In order to heighten the emotional effect which is the primary purpose of your story, you want the reader to identify himself with your viewpoint character. You cannot do this successfully if you keep skipping out of character and sounding like some older person.

When you have decided on your viewpoint character, give him a name and identity. Who is he? What is he? How old is he? Describe his appearance. This description will be mainly for your own edification since you won't have room for it in detail in the space of a short story. But get his appearance clear in your own mind. If Johnny has red freckles on his nose and is sturdily built, see him that way. If Mary has blue eyes and an elfin look about her, get her appearance set in your own imagination. But don't fancy just because you can now see your characters that they are real people. The chances are you still have only a name, an outward shell, perhaps a type. You may have a poor little rich girl, a poor but honest farm boy, a teacher's pet, or a teacher's pest, or any of the hundreds of other categories into which we can pigeonhole characters, young and old. Which is all right. It will help you to see your characters to get them typed. But you won't have people until you individualize within the type. The little orphan girl is certainly a type. But as Doris Gates portrays her in *Sensible Kate* she is a person in her own right and is different from any other orphan in the world.

Living children are made up of so many traits that it would be impossible, even in a novel, to portray one in the full dimensions of life. Not even Tom Sawyer is done as completely as that. It is the writer's task to select such characteristics as will be useful to him in presenting his story. In the case of your main character, one important trait may be chosen, along with two or three lesser traits. If some of these are slightly contradictory, all the better: your character will be more apt to resemble an individual child.

I am asked sometimes if I use real people for my characters. As it happens, I do not. Real people get in my way. If I try to write about a girl I know named Mary Jones, I am likely to find before I am very far into the story that the Mary I know is proving obstinate. Because my characters and plot are so thoroughly interwound I come to a place where, for the sake of the story I want to tell, Mary would have to do or say something which the real Mary would never do or say. And the planning process is balked. So it is better if my Mary is a composite of many little girls I know. Then she can be the kind of person I need for this particular story without in the least flying in the face of reality.

In the case of your viewpoint character, you will have one major advantage and one major disadvantage. You will be able to characterize him through his own thoughts and you will be able to characterize all your other characters by look-ing at them through his eyes and thinking about them with his mind. This is all to the good. As a disadvantage you will not be able to look at your viewpoint character through out-side eyes and you cannot tell what other characters are thinking about him unless they choose to express themselves to him in word, or by action.

Through the eyes of your viewpoint character you will set the scene, give his reactions to that scene, further the action of the story and accomplish many other purposes.

"With the sight of the house her spirits took a sud-den upward zoom and she knew at once why the Tar-rants endured the neighborhood. The structure was more queer than beautiful, perhaps, but it stood out as a real personality among its uninteresting neighbors. It re-minded Ginny of an illustration for a fairy tale and she longed for a pencil and sketch block."

That characterizes both the neighborhood and the girl, and it moves her toward her destination of the house.

Perhaps you are still not altogether willing to concede that you can tell a better story by using a single viewpoint. Per-haps you have been jumping happily around from character to character in your stories and resent having someone rap your knuckles and tell you not to do it any more. All right—let's have a look at a few paragraphs of writing in which the viewpoints are mixed.

Bill glowered at his oatmeal. Ordinarily the stuff was okay, but not when it rained on Saturday. On a rainy Saturday nothing would taste good. The gang had been going to get together and practice football tactics in the

yard that was now being stirred into a big mud pie.
Tony Bryan, one of the boys from high school had
promised to come over and give them all pointers. But
now . . .

Across the table Bill's sister Sally was scraping the
bottom of her bowl. Rainy Saturdays were wonderful.
Mother had promised that on the very next Saturday
it rained she could go up and spend the morning looking through grandmother's trunk in the attic. There
would be wonderful dress-up things in that trunk. It
was too bad Bill was looking so cross, though. Probably
he wouldn't care about the trunk. But how Bill felt
didn't matter. She smiled happily to herself, looking
very pretty with her big blue eyes dancing and her lips
wearing a sunny smile.

Mrs. Hall regarded her two children with mixed emotions. Bill was getting to be more and more of a problem
lately, turning sullen when things didn't go his way. If
only he could be as adaptable and good-natured as Sally.

Old Maria put her head in the dining-room door.
Those kids—dawdling again. Especially that Bill. If he
was *her* son, she'd teach him a little consideration for
his elders. When it rained her bones ached and she
wanted to get her work done and have some time to rest.

The main effect of that story opening is one of confusing
jerks. The first paragraph is fine. This is going to be Bill's
story. The problem is going to concern the fact that it is
raining on a day when he wants to practice football. We begin to be interested. We experience a certain sympathy with
Bill and we want to know what happens.

But in the second paragraph we discover that we were all
wrong. This story is going to be about Sally's morning in the
attic going through her grandmother's trunk. There is a let-
down of interest when we leave Bill's viewpoint and there

is the jerk of an entire change of mood. But being patient souls we rearrange our mental machinery and decide to go along with Sally. At the end of the paragraph about Sally we trip over a sentence about how pretty she looks "with her big blue eyes dancing and her lips wearing a sunny smile." As Sally cannot possibly see herself like this unless she stands before a mirror, we are jerked out of viewpoint again.

In the third paragraph we find that we guessed wrong the first two times and that the story is going to be about Mrs. Hall's problem with Bill and her satisfaction with Sally. At this point the young reader tosses the story down and turns to a comic book because the last problem in the world which is going to interest him is the trouble a mother has with her children.

The grownup reader may keep on to the fourth paragraph where he discovers that the problem has to do with an elderly servant's aching bones on a rainy day. Whereupon even he throws down the story because he is so thoroughly confused that he doesn't know what it is all about, or whom to sympathize with, and cares even less.

Any one of the viewpoints in the above paragraphs might be suitable for a different story, depending upon what story the writer wanted to tell and what kind of audience he meant to write for. But don't cram them all into one story. If I were to be forced to a choice of viewpoint characters for this story, however, I'd say at once that it should be Bill's story if I want to make it a story for children. Everything looks too bright and cheery for Sally for her viewpoint to result in a good story, while Bill is faced with Trouble in paragraph one.

When your viewpoint character is clear in your own mind

you are ready to move on to the rest of the cast. Except that you will not get into the minds of other characters, devices for characterization are about the same for all your people. Major characters may be built up with a fairly lavish hand, while for minor characters you will perhaps select no more than a single trait which will individualize within the type.

There are a number of means by which characters may be made clear to the reader. There are times when straight description must be used. If done badly this can bog down any story. So keep your description fresh and alive.

Remember that matter of immediacy, of something happening now. Don't *tell* the reader. Give him a picture he can see for himself. *Show* your character doing something which characterizes. Don't say, "Midge took her things off in an untidy manner." Get that picture across. Say: "Midge came in, shedding beret, coat and gloves in all directions. She always rid herself of her things with an effect of buttons popping toward every point of the compass."

Dialogue is one of the most useful vehicles for the purpose of characterization. Yet in so many first stories all the characters sound exactly alike. Make the words your people speak bear out whatever traits of character you have chosen for them. If your heroine is a gay young person, don't talk about it—make her sound gay. If a boy character is deep in gloom like Bill facing a rainy Saturday, then he certainly mustn't sound exactly like your cheery heroine, or vice versa.

Like Alice, most of us prefer to find lots of conversation in the stories we read. A solid page of print, unbroken by dialogue is tiresome to the eye. What people say is just as important as what they do and every bit as interesting. It is immediately a key to character, if handled properly, and will give the illusion of reality so necessary to a satisfying story.

The most important rule in the writing of dialogue is to make it sound natural. An ear for dialogue is a valuable asset to any writer and you can develop such an ear if you listen carefully enough.

It is not always easy for an adult to make young people in a story sound the way they really do in life. You need to spend considerable time listening to children as they talk today before you can do it successfully. Remembering is not good enough because speech idiom changes with the passing of years. Check your own slang habits and don't permit in your story phrases which were commonly used when you were a child. Just because they sound natural to you, does not mean that they will be understood by today's youngsters, let alone used by them.

In the matter of slang, a moderate amount may be used to give naturalness to conversation, but it is wiser to avoid the short-lived catch phrase of the moment. It may be dated by the time your story sees print, and in a book is likely to seem archaic in a year or two. In a recent story I had a character refer to "the sixty-four dollar question." At the time of writing there were few youngsters in America who would not understand that phrase. But how long it would be meaningful was a matter of conjecture. I decided to delete it.

Apparently young people are going to go on saying "swell" forever and a day. No amount of discouragement from their elders has so far done away with the habit. However much frowned upon in some quarters (mainly because it is used

unimaginatively to denote practically anything agreeable),
it is a part of today's language and can at times be used
effectively in the mouth of some story character.

Discretion, good judgment, good taste (but not too sissy
a taste) must guide you in this matter of slang. Profanity
has been taboo in stories for young people and is still very
much so in the magazine field. Occasionally these days this
type of realism will be found in books for older boys. I remember a case where a hardboiled Marine was supposed to
use a phrase actually used in Marine parlance. To take out
the naughty word and make that Marine a sissy would
certainly have lost the story illusion.

By all means read your dialogue aloud. It is good practice,
of course, to read your entire story aloud. A good many
wordings which look pleasant enough in type can be found
awkward, or rather silly when spoken aloud. Use shortened
forms, loosen up your character's speech, avoid stiffness and
formality. Keep to the words each character would be likely
to use. And show by the things a character says what manner of person he is.

It is a good exercise to check the dialogue in the stories of
skilled writers and study how well character may be revealed
through speech.

There are a few minor matters to watch. Just as solid
pages of unbroken print are tiresome to the eye, so long passages of dialogue spoken by one character can be equally
tiresome. In the course of ordinary conversation few children make long stump speeches without interruption. If it
is necessary for a character to tell a long story, have other
characters break in from time to time, or interrupt the talk

with some bit of action. Never let your character get up on a soap box.

Don't be afraid of "cueing" your dialogue. "He said" is a perfectly good phrase, but some writers become so afraid of repeating it that they go to fantastic lengths to substitute other words. It is annoying to a reader to follow a page where the author has used in rotation, "he admitted," "she confided," "he enjoined," "she hazarded," "he boasted," "she mimicked," and so on. The reader begins to long for just one simple "said." It is true that too many "saids" in a row can also intrude, but they are to be preferred to the above method.

Perhaps the best method is to use "saids" and occasional "said" substitutes, arriving at variety by rearranging your sentence structure.

Don't always use the common form: "I'm awfully sorry about being late again, Mrs. Farmer," Mary Blake said, coming down from her high horse in a split second.

Try it this way: Mary Blake came down from her high horse in a split second. "I'm awfully sorry about being late again, Mrs. Farmer."

Above all, don't use grotesque substitutes. Don't write, "I think the drawing is beautiful," Polly beamed. I'd like to see anyone *beam* a sentence. If you want to write something of that sort, be very sure there is a period after the word "beautiful."

The important thing is not to leave your reader in the dark as to which character is speaking. Even when there are only two people on the scene it can become very confusing after a few speeches if the author does no cueing.

It is a valuable help to start collecting juvenile characters in that notebook you carry around in your pocket or purse. Don't put down a feature-by-feature description of the little girl sitting across from you on the train. It doesn't matter that she has blue eyes and blond hair. Look for the *significant*. Do her eyes examine her fellow passengers with lively interest? Or does her attention dart here and there in a frightened way? Is her blond hair limp and bedraggled, or has someone brushed it into shining smoothness? These are the things which give you the significant, characterizing detail. She is wearing brown sandals, perhaps. Nothing significant about that. But let the sandals be polished to brilliance despite scuffed toes, and the socks mended but clean and we have some idea of the child's background. So on through every detail of appearance and manner. What is her voice like? How does she stand? How does she walk? What can you read about her from all these signs?

It will take a little patience at first, a little practice, but if you stay with it you'll develop a knack for distinguishing the significant at a glance and you'll have a wealth of material to draw from when you need it.

We learn to characterize, not only by watching others, but by observing ourselves. No day of our lives passes without our being stirred to some emotion. We are pleased, annoyed, embarrassed, moved to tears or laughter. Get the habit of looking at yourself objectively and finding out what makes you click. Was your impatience justified? Why were you so ridiculously pleased over that casual word of praise? Or unreasonably hurt by so small a slight? Understand these things in yourself and you will be better able to understand your characters. Emotions are not very different, whether you are writing about children or grownups. They are simpler and more spontaneous in childhood, perhaps. Joys are more keen, disappointments more cutting. But out of your own joys and disappointments you learn to understand the emotions of your characters.

When you want to portray an unpleasant character, try giving him some of your own faults. Our faults as adults had their beginnings when we were children. We can see the unpleasant aspect of those faults and at the same time understand why they came into being and what difficulties they may cause. As a result, your young character is more likely to be human and believable. Oddly enough, in the questionnaire given out to writing classes, we always come upon some few students who say they are not aware of possessing any bad habits. Our recommendation to these lucky individuals is to give up writing. Your faults are part of your stock in trade as a writer, and this is one place where they can stand you in good stead. Better recognize and utilize them.

Conversely, here is your opportunity to extoll all those virtues you felt went unappreciated by dull grownups when you were a child. There is a universality about good behavior and bad which belongs to both the juvenile and the adult world. We feel very much the same emotions a child feels, but we have learned to control and repress until we are less primitive about them. The fundamental psychological needs we knew as children grew up with us and became the adult.

Let us say that by now you have your characters drawn up clearly in your own mind. You are nearly ready to set them down on paper in a story. Don't begin writing until you have decided what role each character is to play in your reader's emotions. This may seem so obvious that you are likely to dismiss the advice as something you already know. Are you sure you know?

You say you want your reader to be sympathetically inclined toward Mary Jones; that the emotions you wish to arouse are liking, tolerant amusement, turning finally into admiration at the close of the story. However, on page six your fictional little girl steps completely out of character and reveals a flash of bad temper for which you had not prepared your reader and which loses for her the liking you had meant to build up.

"But," you say, "I am only making her a human little girl. I thought I was supposed to give her contradictory traits."

Right. You were. But see to it that those contradictory traits still contribute to the general impression you want to make upon the reader. Her faults had better be minor ones; she can be mistaken in her views, or in some action she takes, but she mustn't be petty and bad-tempered. Not if you want to keep her sympathetic throughout the story, and build up to the admiration you want for this particular little girl at the end.

Another thing: Don't set your characters down in a void. Richness of background is one of the most useful means of bringing a story to life. By "richness" I don't mean the sumptuous. I mean richness of sensory detail. Background may help to characterize your people, either by suiting them, or by contrasting incongruously. There is something challenging to the interest about a well-dressed girl in a shabby setting, or a shabby girl against a luxurious background, and the very contrast will serve to characterize when we learn the why behind it.

Too often a beginner's stories take place in a vacuum and

he forgets entirely about appealing to the reader's senses. This is important enough in writing for grownups, but in children's stories it is imperative. Children understand much of what goes on about them through their senses, and skillful writers use sensory detail to a marked degree in writing for young people. Always keep these sense aids in mind and use as many as possible in your writing. Not in long, heavy paragraphs of description, but by weaving them unobtrusively through your action and dialogue.

Characterization is not something you do when one of your story people first walks on the stage. In story after story by beginners, flat statements are to be found. A character is tall, dark and handsome; he has laughing eyes and gleaming teeth (or is it the other way around?), but thereafter all "characterizing" touches are abandoned for the remainder of the story. He becomes an invisible nonentity who makes speeches that sound just like all the speeches made by other nonentities whom we distinguish one from another, male or female, young or old, only by name.

Characterization is something you do *consistently* with every character every time he appears on a scene.

That word *"consistently"* is the most important word in the rule. Perhaps more than any other one fault inconsistency of characterization will bring rejection slips. In the early part of a story Johnny is a mule-stubborn little boy who wants what he wants—or else. At the climax he yields amiably to the desires of another character, at no little cost to himself. And the editor writes "characterization not consistent" on a rejection slip and sends it back. It isn't that Johnny could not change in the course of a story, providing the character change and the reason behind it are carefully

developed along the way. But when a character does a broad
jump from here to yon for no other reason than to suit the
author's whim, then characterization is certainly inconsistent.

This is where that measuring stick I mentioned some time
ago comes in. The test is a simple one to make, but it is
tremendously important. Take each paragraph of your story
in turn and analyze it. What characters are on the scene at
that point? Does that paragraph individualize each young
person each time he appears? Does it contribute in some way
to the reader's understanding of him as a person? Is it *consistent?*

If your hero is a tough little egg on page one, only to sound
like a sissy on page two, you aren't visualizing him very
clearly yourself and you are certainly confusing your reader.
If you find that your colors have blurred and all your characters
have run together in an indistinguishable mass, then
sit down and introduce consistent characterization throughout
the story.

No character must be goody-goody, no character must be
thoroughly black. No living child belongs to either extreme.
Look for faults in your good characters and see that your
bad ones have virtues, and you'll be much more likely to
write about children as they are.

Again I'd like to warn that as much as possible grown up
characters should be kept off the scene. Your young readers
are interested in young characters, and they don't give a
whoop about Aunt Josie's romance, or about the disaster
that is about to befall Uncle Ned. *Not unless those things
very strongly affect their own interests.* Above all, whether
you are writing a short story or a book, get your major characters
into the scene as early as you possibly can. Don't drag
them in by their heels at the last minute because you need

them in the climax scene. Recently a book manuscript came to me for criticism in which the hero of this teen-age story for girls came into the story when the book was three-quarters over. I protested and the author told me that the hero really wasn't "very important." But your teen-age reader wants a hero who *is* important, and she wants to know about him right away. It may not be that his importance is recognized immediately, but he should certainly be in evidence from the first.

There is one final warning and in this matter no one can help you. You can do almost mechanically all the things I have set down in this chapter. They will help you to make your children real. But there is one bit of magic which only you can breathe into this collection of features and traits you build up and name and call a character.

Somehow, before your straw man comes to life, you must by empathy get yourself into his skin. Empathy, according to Rebecca West's definition, is "our power of projecting ourselves into the destiny of others by fantasy."

I have gone through the disheartening experience of drawing up a character who should have carried a conviction of life, but who somehow behaved in a forced and wooden manner when he stepped out on my story stage. I had not succeeded in projecting myself into his destiny. This I cannot tell you how to do. I only know that it must be done and that all these other things will help greatly to put you in a position where you can work the final magic yourself. Then the young people who take up your story will read with delight, knowing they are meeting other youngsters as real as themselves; new friends they will want to keep for old friends, whose experiences they will profit by long after they have put your story down.

IX

The Chicken or the Egg:
2. THE EGG, PLOT

All the while that you are working with your characters plot material will be coming to life, almost without effort. The desire and characteristics of one character clash with those of another and plot ideas begin to develop. On the other hand, when you begin to work directly with plot you will find that your situations, your story problem, your theme, all require certain types of character to handle them. It is quite likely that the exigencies of your plot will cause you to rework some of your characters.

It is equally likely as your characters come to life and new plot incidents develop, you may want to change the framework of your plan. One affects the other, both are interwoven, and it is foolish to try to choose between the chicken and the egg.

By all means, while you are planning your story—even while you are writing it—keep your material flexible. Don't feel that you are making a plaster cast with rigid outlines from which you must never depart. Within the boundaries of certain laws which you will be wiser to allow to govern your story-telling, feel always that you can change anything anywhere along the line. Don't reject the new idea which your subconscious suddenly provides you with. Make it welcome and see if it might not improve your story, even if it is something which did not come into your first planning.

Quite often a plotting impasse grows out of planning too rigidly and tying ourselves into such knots that we miss seeing the loose end lying right at hand which we have only to tug to untie everything. I recall the difficulties one writer got himself into simply because he required a window at a certain point in his story through which a character could make an escape. When the use of such a window was pointed out to him, he regarded his critic blankly, protesting that no such window existed in the building he had in mind. His imaginary conception of the scene was so clear in his mind that he forgot it was up to him as the creator to put a window wherever he wanted one. It is fine to see things as vividly as that, but not to the extent that it blinds and hampers you when it comes to changes that need to be made.

Plot, as a rule, is the bugaboo of every beginner. The word seems to imply the need of some very special knack, some highly developed skill. All the other elements of writing appear easy to learn, but an ogre of grimmest mien guards the mysterious gateway to plotting. And right before that entrance a good many writers lay down their pens and flee.

Which is very silly indeed because the ogre is quite imaginary. A plot is only a plan—a method of organizing your material so that it will accomplish the things you want a story to do: that is, to interest and move the reader. This takes a little discipline, a bit of practice, but once you understand the matter, it should never defeat you again. To reach an audience, any art needs an understandable form. A plot, a plan, will give you that form.

Of course it is your old friend down in the subconscious who is conjuring up this apparition with which to frighten you away. The grim determination with which you have (I trust) been digging into this writing business has him really worried. He knows a lot better than you do that this is where *he* goes to work. This is his last chance to discourage you and if he doesn't do a good job of it he will find his reluctant little nose held right to that grindstone he dreads.

So up he comes with this fearful ogre. "You can't possibly plot," he whispers. "Who do you think you are? Besides, it takes a crass commercial sense to work out mechanical stuff like that. You are an Artist. You can create character. You can write the most luscious descriptions. But plotting—ah, no, keep your hands free of anything so low-brow as that. Besides, you couldn't anyway, even if you tried."

Right there is where you fling his words back in his face and pay no attention to any snappy comeback he may hand you. Anyone with a moderate amount of intelligence and imagination can learn to plan a story. The only terrifying thing about it is that this is the place where you really have to go to work and *think*. You have to concentrate intensively. If your early training has prepared you for this you have an ace in your favor. If you find that when you start trying to think about your plot, your mind gets off on the grocery list, or that tooth that ought to be filled, or where you mean to spend your next vacation, or any number of other irrelevant matters, you are going to have to do a little persistent training right now. So let's get on with it.

Have a clock at hand. Make yourself comfortable. My choice is to stretch out on a couch at full length if I want to "plot" during the day. Sometimes I do it just before I go to sleep at night, but my purpose then is a little different and the thinking at night must be approached with some caution or you will find yourself so wide awake that you won't get to sleep for hours.

The clock is necessary in the beginning for training purposes. Later you can dispense with it. At first you will need to time yourself in order to hold your mind sternly to the matter in hand. The first day you are going to think for at least five minutes straight about your story. It will be harder than you imagine. Every time the grocery list or anything else tries to crowd in, you are going to push it right out of your consciousness and pull your attention back to that story. Every time your mind wanders, start your five minutes over again, until you get in an uninterrupted stretch. Increase your time from day to day with respect to the progress you make.

It is a help, I think, to close your eyes, even to put your palms over your eyes until you see nothing but black. *Think* black for a few seconds. Whisper the word "black" over and over until there is nothing in your mind but soothing darkness. Then turn on the film and start watching your story people act out a scene. When you have practiced this intensive concentration over a period of several weeks, months, years, you will find that you can turn that story reel on whenever you want to and hold your attention to it for as long a time as you care to spend. After a while you won't need to go through the rigmarole of closing your eyes or lying down; you'll find you can do it any time at all. You can do it while you're scrubbing in the tub, or riding on a street car, or—if you don't watch out—while you're crossing the street in the midst of weaving traffic. You are likely to cut your best friends dead on the street because you are far away in your story and don't even see them, and you are likely to increase your already growing reputation for being odd, but that's all right: this is plotting.

It is not something which can be done in an hour or two. It is not something which can be pushed or hurried. It is something which grows and develops gradually as you feed more and more ideas to your subconscious. They will be jelling while you aren't thinking about them at all; they'll be growing while you sleep.

Every day you sort over the new material with which your subconscious has provided you in return for the odds and ends you have fed it, and see what you can do by way of fitting it into a prescribed story pattern. When your mind balks and a scene refuses to develop, it may mean that you have been trying to force your material into an unnatural pattern which the subconscious is rejecting. Try to get a new slant on that particular scene or problem, a new approach. Examine all its elements, explore new paths it may take. The trouble may only be that at this point you have not doled out enough new and stimulating story germs, so that your mind hasn't enough to work on to develop the scene. If that is the case, it is a good idea to read a book about the subject you're working on, or get out into the field and see what imagination-stimulating data you can collect.

When some problem really stumps me, I resort to thinking about it just before I go to sleep. I do *not* try to figure it out completely at that time because I know only too well that would only wake me up and probably would not solve the difficulty at all. I spend a few minutes impressing my problem upon my little subconscious pal. I tell him quietly that to-morrow I am going to find that difficulty solved. I hold my-self to that line of thought as nearly as possible without wavering until I fall asleep.

I don't want to be esoteric or wave black magic wands under your nose, but if there is any magic to this matter of being a writer, it rests in the use you make of your subconscious. The above-mentioned method is, of course, psychologically sound, and has been proved so many times by people in almost every line of work that it needs no apology or defense.

Don't try to beat your mind into doing this work for you. It isn't necessary to be grimly determined about it. Nor can you approach it with doubt and despair. Quiet confidence is the attitude which you must achieve. You must know without any doubt that this will work, and you must fall asleep repeating your conviction over and over in your mind.

When morning comes, don't expect to be awakened by trumpets which announce that the answer has been provided. Don't expect any blinding revelations. In fact, it is possible that the next time you think of the matter the problem will look just as knotty as ever. Then you go back to your desk and you recall some vague idea that you'd touched on uncertainly yesterday; you find that today it sounds more sensible. You get to work and without any fanfare, perhaps without conscious realization on your part, the matter works itself out. You may even say, "But I had that in mind all along. It wasn't any subconscious nonsense that figured that out." Nevertheless, yesterday you were stuck, and today you are going ahead.

It doesn't always happen as quickly as that. Sometimes

it may take much longer than twenty-four hours. Sometimes you may have to put that particular problem aside (with instructions to your helper to come up with something later on) and turn your immediate attention to some other angle of your story, or even to another story. But sooner or later, unless you are forcing something very much against the grain, the answer will appear and you'll be over another hump.

I find it a help, even when my next scene is so thoroughly planned that no problem exists, to try to fall asleep knowing that I will be able to handle that scene satisfactorily when I return to my typewriter the next morning.

At first all this must be employed by making a special effort. After a while, like the other elements of story writing, it will become so much a part of your working method that you will do it automatically without thinking much about it except on such occasions when your material turns unusually stubborn.

So much for the "hard" part of plotting. The rest is easy because it is technical and mechanical. There are certain things you must accomplish in every story you write. Once you understand these matters, you will have no particular difficulty fitting your material into the best possible form.

There are many ways in which you may put your story together. At this point dogma of any kind is dangerous. One writer's method, however sound and sensible, may not work for another. In the beginning, if you can train yourself to one of the better, time-saving methods, you may save yourself a great deal of grief later on. When you become thoroughly conditioned to a writing method and then try to force yourself into a different pattern of work, you may be halted and inhibited so that your imagination will not work at all.

Some people think easily of climax scenes first and then work backward to get an opening and the rest of the preceding scenes. Others take no interest whatsoever in climaxes until they have thought through all the beginning steps.

But however you start putting things together, try to make an outline first. There are writers who work by the sit-down-and-dash-it-off method, but usually they have the kind of fast-moving minds in which some sort of outline is dashing on ahead of the scene in hand and is ready when they come to it. Really good workers who write by this method are rare, and second-rate stories turned out by this group show the lack of planning which has gone into them.

I won't quarrel with your manner of outlining, so long as you do outline. Some writers work best with an outline which is completely mental. Others like to do it thoroughly on paper. Still others get results by talking it over with someone else. All three methods have advantages and disadvantages and you may work out a combination of the three.

The "mental" outline has an advantage in that it does not take the edge off the writing itself. If you can think your story through *completely* from beginning to end, you are almost sure to approach the writing with a feeling of freshness and adventure. Unfortunately this type of outline is apt to get a little blurred around the edges because you rush over some troublesome point that is not down on paper to stare you accusingly in the eye. Then you start writing, reach that point and stick right there. All your interest in the story dies out, you become bored with it, and unless you exert a great deal of discipline, you will find yourself putting it aside as a failure and going on to some fresher and more appealing idea. It is all too easy to become a "beginner" and not a "finisher." If you are troubled by this drop in interest a few pages after the start of your story, the difficulty probably lies in a lack of careful planning. The mental outline, like any other, is good only if it is complete. For a book it is scarcely to be considered because it would be impossible for most minds to hold such a bulk of material in view by that method.

The written outline is undoubtedly the best. Some writers claim that once they have worked over an outline they feel they have written the story and all their zest for the actual writing is gone. There is something in this, and I remember very well using the same excuse myself. Mainly, however, I believe that it is a matter of poor conditioning. I can do a great deal of outlining now without having it interfere in the least with the writing of the story. You will be better off if you condition yourself to working with an outline.

In the matter of "talking it over," I'd like to issue words of warning. It can be very helpful to talk over various aspects of a story with certain people whose judgment you can trust and whose views are sympathetic, though not necessarily always in agreement with yours. I believe, however, that you can do this safely only when you have the confidence of success behind you. Nothing anyone can say will then throw you so completely off that you cannot write the story.

With the beginner this may easily happen. I have seen too many books go into the discard simply because the writers talked about them too much while they were writing them. One person gives you one angle, another contradicts the first, and as many views on a subject can be found as there are people to talk to. Wet blankets are thrown out carelessly, and the result for the writer may be a state of such confusion that he cannot write that book at all. This can be just as true with parts of a short story. It is sometimes safer to get it down, get it done—then do your talking and tearing apart. This may seem wasteful as to time, but at least you will have a finished piece of work to look at, and if necessary, reassemble, instead of being thrown off to such an extent that you can't work at all.

However you manage it—outline! If you don't, you are very likely to find yourself painting a lovely shade of blue on a wall that does not exist, or building a fireplace with no chimney above it, or getting your house completed, only to find that you've forgotten the stairs. Then it will take a real tearing down to rebuild.

After all, you can't put up so much as your front door unless you know whether you mean to build a firehouse, a grocery store, or a Hollywood mansion. Your outline gives you the blueprint for your house and settles a great many matters before you get to the point of laying the cornerstone.

What you feed your imagination first in the matter of building a plot, does not very much matter. It may be a character, a theme, a situation, a setting, a job, a hobby, anything at all. But once you get the thing stirring, with bits coming to life here and there, you must decide definitely and clearly on your story problem. What is it your main character wants? How much depends on his success? What events and people oppose him? (It must never be easy for him or you'll have no suspense.) What does he do to overcome these obstacles? How does he *by his own action* solve his problem? When you have answered those questions you have a "plot."

It's as hard as that. If you leave any of them unanswered, or omitted, your story framework will not be strong enough and someone will tell you you lack a plot.

Suppose we look at these questions individually with special regard to writing for young people.

What is it your main character wants? Give him something he wants very much. Make his problem sympathetic to the interests of the reader-age for which you intend your story. Make it an important want, not one that is cheap or trivial. A young girl who wants to learn to be liked can be made a very sympathetic character. But a girl who merely wants to be the belle of the ball so she can take the attention of the boys away from the other girls has a motive so petty that she does not deserve the dignity of being made the heroine of a story. Don't, however, make your main character's desire so noble and laudatory that it has very little connection with real young people (however admirable it may seem to grownups), or you will lose your audience on page one.

How much depends on your main character's getting what he wants? It must *matter*. Your reader must care what happens because so many unhappy things will result if the character fails that his sympathies as a reader will be bent on seeing your hero achieve his aim.

What events and people oppose him? It must never be easy. Getting your character into continual hot water is one of the secrets of suspense. So much must stack up against him that the possibility of success will look very dubious at several points in the story. If your girl who wants to be liked decides to be more pleasant, more interested in other people, and then goes right out and gets herself liked by being more pleasant and interested, you have no obstacles to your problem, no conflict, no story.

Having decided on the obstacles, what does your main character do to overcome them? How does your boy hero reveal whatever admirable characteristics you have given him in his course of struggle for success? Of course before one obstacle is overcome another must raise its head, so that your reader is carried along from scene to scene, always wanting to know what will happen next. The moment you leave him satisfied, with no further questions arising in his mind, your story is over, whether you want it to be or not.

How does he finally *by his own action* solve his problem? This is important. Too often problems are solved by fortuity, by chance. Somebody else happens along and saves the day, getting your hero neatly out of his scrape. But if your hero is going to be one, he has to get out of his own scrapes. Luck can play a greater part in real life than it can in fiction.

If something just happens, if he doesn't do it himself, your story will not carry a fully satisfying climax. And if there is no other rule to be regarded in writing for children, this one must be—the ending must satisfy. Writers for little magazines may take the lazy way and end everything with gloom and disaster. It is much easier to leave your reader with the feeling that All is Futility than it is to work out a satisfactory solution that helps to give him the confidence to go ahead and solve his own problems.

This final solution must come through *character action*. Because of the sort of person you have made your leading character he performs some action which solves the problem. He doesn't run into something someone else does which makes him "come to realize" that he has been mistaken and must be a better boy from now on. Avoid these come-to-realize solutions as you would poison. They are not dramatic and they seldom satisfy.

In a sense, perhaps, all stories which show character change have come-to-realize plots. The point which must be kept in mind is that the character comes to this state of realization out of his own action—not because someone else tells him he must do better, so that he merely changes his mind.

To understand this we might look at a book for older girls —*Gateway* by Amelia Elizabeth Walden. Peyton Marshall, the book's secondary heroine, is the spoiled daughter of a wealthy businessman and a famous movie star. Peyton is selfish, sarcastic, unscrupulous about taking away other girls' boy friends, and thoroughly unpleasant in every way. Naturally, she is a dissatisfied, unhappy young woman. But so skillful is the author's characterization that the reader understands why Peyton is as she is. Thus she does not become an unsympathetic character, but rather one to be pitied, and one who possesses enough good characteristics to make the reader want to see her change.

During the course of the story a boy Peyton admires tells her how all wrong she is and urges her to change. If, at this point, Peyton took his advice and reformed because of it, the story would have a weak come-to-realize plot. In life it usually takes a lot more than merely telling people to get them to change. They need to learn the hard way—by the consequences of their own wrong actions. Up to the climax of the story Peyton is still going her own wrong-headed way. Then, because of the disastrous results which are piling up through her behavior, she begins to see the light. But even then she does not sit down and say she will try to be a better girl. There would be nothing dramatic about that, and again it would weaken the story. She *takes action*. In this case rather heroic action which makes amends for the harm she has done to herself and others. Come-to-realize plots seem to grow on every bush. If you have one growing in your own typewriter, check it against the above pattern and be sure your main character learns from his own action and then takes further action of his own.

There must, of course, be action in stories for young people. By "action" we don't mean that something wildly exciting must happen on every page. What we mean is a sense of something happening and the underlying promise that more is about to happen. This can often be achieved in a scene where there is no physical action going on at all.

Think of your story as a series of scenes being presented on a stage. In your planning, break it up into four or five parts, each, if possible, laid against a different background. A change of scene may mean no more than a shift to another room, but it always adds interest to the story. If your transitions are quickly and smoothly accomplished these changes of background will give your story a flowing movement that carries it on toward the climax. It may be necessary to return at times to a scene previously presented, but usually there is a difference as to time of day or people present which will keep it from being repetitive. A story which begins in one room and continues in that same setting to the end of the story can be very monotonous.

The time element must be considered in your planning. In a short story don't begin when your heroine was three years old and have her grow up in the first few pages so that your story covers a long period of years. Very few stories cannot be improved by starting them within the fewest possible hours of your climax. Two or three days may well be sufficient time for your story to happen, though of course your material will guide you to a great extent in this. Usually, however, all that vital information that makes you want to start the action several months or years before the climax, can be woven into the first paragraphs if you give enough thought and effort to the matter.

In your planning, watch always for the trite and the obvious and reject them for something more unusual. The idea that comes most easily is to be regarded with suspicion. Your subconscious helper is merely trying to put one over on you. He has read that same idea in so many stories that he doesn't have to work at all to present you with it. When you say, "Come, come, produce!" he reaches for the nearest shelf and hands you whatever is closest, hoping you will be happy with it and let him go back to sleep. But you're going to hand it right back to him. You're going to say sternly, "I've seen this before. It is so shopworn nobody wants it, including me. So get busy and dig back a little farther into the storeroom and get me something nice and fresh."

You are the boss, you know, if you get off to the right start.

Before concluding this chapter on plot I want to return to that plot notebook I mentioned some chapters back as being one book I kept up faithfully all through my short story writing days. Almost anything that will provide an idea may go into that book. You may have a section for themes, for characters, for unusual hobbies—anything at all that may stimulate your imagination. But I kept more than these in my book; I kept a list of plot situations that ran into the hundreds and from which I could always draw when the well began to run dry.

If you are going to write for children, you must of course keep reading stories and books written for them by others. This will help to keep you in the mood, in the "swing." From every story or book I read at this period I separated the germinal situation, free of all its story trappings, and set it down in my book. Scanning a few pages, I find such items as the following:

A girl sets out to teach someone a lesson and learns the same lesson herself.

A girl discovers that you can't dislike people, once you get to know them. (*This simple truth is the theme of* Willow Hill, *which won me a prize.*)

A girl is so intent upon a goal she wants to reach that she misses the fact that it is more important to enjoy the road which leads to that goal.

A group of young people find themselves in desperate circumstances, only to have one of their number whom they have previously scorned, provide the way out.

You can make your own list. Boil every story you read down to the very germ that tells what it is about. You are not going to be interested in how that particular writer worked the story out; in fact, you must be very sure that you follow no one else's beaten path, or you will be plagiarizing. Collect so many of these plot situations that you forget what the original stories were about. Then, when you are in need of a story idea, feed a few of them to your imagination and see what clicks. A hundred writers could take the above situations and write a hundred stories that would in no way resemble one another. The possibilities are limitless. When you use this method, you can start off happily with the first step taken toward your plot. You can write down in one sentence what your story is going to be about—which should always be your first step in story writing.

Another section of your notebook may be given over to "opening situations." These may resemble the germinal plots to some extent, but there is a difference, since these will present you with your opening scene ready-made. Here are two from my collection:

A young librarian is feeling hemmed in by books, longing for wider horizons and more contact with life.

A girl comes home to a situation where she knows she isn't wanted.

These, like the others, can go on forever and it is more stimulating to collect your own. The one about the librarian served as my opening situation in *The Silver Inkwell*. The girl who felt hemmed in wanted to write books, instead of just handing them over a counter.

Another advantage in starting off with a situation lies in the fact that you are immediately presented with two or more characters. All you need to do is start getting acquainted with them and find out why that situation faces them and what they mean to do about it.

However you manage it, keep the idea reservoir constantly replenished and don't let the ogre of plot frighten you. If you keep your subconscious well-fed with story ideas, if you plan your story carefully so that the questions named in this chapter are answered, you need have little worry about learning to plot.

X

CASE STORY:
STORM OVER THE ART LEAGUE*

By

Phyllis A. Whitney

There were just three steps leading to the basement recreation room of the Poplar City public library, and Jinny Somerset managed to fall down all three.

It was the big gilt frame on Bonita's picture that caused her undoing. She'd had the thing balanced securely enough, but it had cut off her view of the stairs and in feeling for the top step her foot slipped and down the short flight she went with a tremendous clatter.

Five of the leading members of the Young People's Art League, who were spending their evening hanging exhibition pictures, rushed to the double doors and watched her unscramble herself. Larry Bendock's tall figure headed the group.

"I'm not hurt," Jinny said quickly as she saw their shocked expressions.

Larry looked relieved. "Don't touch her till she's counted her bones," he warned. "There's no use picking her up if she's going to fall apart on our hands."

* Reprinted by Permission of *The American Girl,* Magazine For All Girls, Published by The Girl Scouts. (Issue of September, 1942).

[A.]† Jinny blushed and was annoyed with herself for doing so. Why did life always play tricks like this? Here she'd wanted to sneak that picture in quietly before anyone knew what she was up to—and then this had to happen!

Through the open door she could see a stepladder with Diane Chalmers perched picturesquely at its top, and the contrast between Diane and herself added still more to her discomfort.

Diane's smock was immaculate and exactly matched the blue of her eyes. Every fair curl was in place and she looked, as usual, as pretty as the charming little water colors she loved to paint.

Jinny had had to rush home from work, change hurriedly, and dash for the library, and she had a sad suspicion how she herself looked at that particular moment. Her green smock, faded by many tubbings, still bore evidence of a paint-mongering past. What was worse, a corner of that gilt atrocity had torn a huge rent in her sleeve in the course of the tumble. She knew her dark hair was mussed, and she could just glimpse the smudge on her nose. Which gave her a decided sense of disadvantage beside the glamorous Diane.

She took Larry's hand and pulled herself to her feet. In spite of the damage to her external person, all bones were at least intact. Bonita's picture was intact, too, and had suffered only a slight chipping of gilt from its impressive frame.

The others went back to their picture hanging, but Larry lingered a moment, looking her over with critical eyes.

"The only suggestion I have to offer concerns your lack of technique," he said pleasantly. "The accepted way of

† For references to letters see next chapter.

tumbling downstairs with a picture is to get your head stuck through the frame."

[B.] Jinny made a face at him and took up her burden, holding the water color carefully hidden against her smock.

[C.] Larry ambled back into the room, lazy and comfortable in his gray slacks and blue shirt. But Jinny had learned long ago that his apparent indolence hid an energy that was inexhaustible, and her resolve to enlist him on her side in the matter of Bonita's picture increased.

There was a long table at one end of the room and she carried the water color over and rested it on its top, with the face still hidden. Trouble lay ahead and she might as well sail right into it. "You'd better save wall space for one more," she said to the room in general.

Diane sighed and waved the hammer, which she was using in the manner of a director's baton, at a square of wall space. "That's the last inch of room. All entries were supposed to be in by yesterday."

"I had to take this away from Bonita Giorno practically by force," Jinny explained. "She wasn't going to enter it. Her mother took a family portrait off the living room wall to furnish a frame."

"Bonita Giorno?" Diane echoed, and Jinny knew what was coming.

[D.] "Bonita was left out of our last exhibit," she said steadily. "I think she ought to be included this time."

Diane raised her lovely eyebrows in surprise. "She was left out because she hasn't the least bit of talent. All her art teachers say she did awful work in school. I don't think people like that ought to be encouraged."

Jinny's hands tightened on the gilt frame until she could feel the ugly leaf design embedding itself in her palms. The one thing she mustn't do was get into an open feud with Diane.

"There are three of us on the committee to judge the work submitted," she said, keeping her voice firm by an effort. "I'm casting my vote for Bonita's picture."

"You need two votes," Diane pointed out. "If Larry and I vote against it, it's out."

Jinny looked toward Larry and her heart sank. He sat straddling a camp chair, his arms folded along its back, his eyes fixed on Diane. Jinny longed to go over and shake him. She wanted to say, "Sure, Diane's lovely to look at, and her uncle's the famous children's illustrator, Burgess Chalmers, and she does pretty-pretty water colors of pretty-pretty scenes, but what's she really *got?*"

But she knew it wouldn't do any good. Diane was romantically lovely and she lent a very special touch to the otherwise grubby and industrious little art group which Larry himself had organized. Diane had even prevailed upon Burgess Chalmers to come to Poplar City tomorrow night to judge the exhibit and award the prizes—and that in itself seemed to entitle her to the role of crown princess.

"All right, let's have your votes," Jinny said, but her hope of success was ebbing. If only she'd been able to get that picture in without attracting attention, so that everyone could have become acquainted with it before a discussion was raised. A picture like Bonita's grew on you sometimes, after you got used to it. But her ridiculous fiasco on the stairs had gained her a spotlight she didn't want.

"Let's have a look at it," Larry said, and reluctantly, Jinny turned the picture around.

The room was completely quiet, and she could see the various expressions of disapproval and bewilderment.

Bonita Giorno, who had never seen the sea, had done a seascape. She had put into the painting some of her own stormy young emotions. It had violence, it had mood—and it was a complete rebellion against the accepted in composition and technique. In the eyes of Poplar City it was definitely not Art.

"You see," Jinny said hurriedly, avoiding the eyes of the room, "she'd read a story by Joseph Conrad and—"

"I'm sorry," Diane interrupted in the gentle tone one might use to a lunatic, "but I'm afraid I couldn't vote for a picture like that. It just goes to prove what I was saying about Bonita's lack of talent."

"Larry," Jinny said, and she tried to put into that one word a plea for understanding. She and Larry had been friends long before Diane came to town, and he was the one person who might get her point of view.

But he shook his head. "I'll have to give it my blackball, too. You ought to know better, Jinny, than to bring over a daub like that."

Her impulse was to pick up the picture and walk haughtily out of the room. But that would mean giving up her championship of Bonita Giorno, and Bonita, whether she realized it or not, needed a champion. There was still one chance left.

"I never expected to see Larry Bendock turn into an artistic snob," Jinny said lightly and waited, knowing Larry.

He flushed a little, but grinned at her. "Nobody gets away with calling *me* an artistic snob. Better explain yourself, young lady."

"Give me a lift back to Bonita's with this and I will," she said.

[E.] But when he'd risen to the bait and they were in his car, she scarcely knew where to begin. Explaining anything like this was so difficult.

"You know what a howl there'd be, if that picture were hung," Larry told her reasonably as they set off for the other side of the tracks. "We've had a tough enough time, trying to get this town to pay some attention to the art group as it is, without going out of our way to look for trouble."

Jinny said sternly, "You never used to be afraid of trouble. Bonita has more than any of us, so far as talent goes, but she's not getting a fair chance to develop it because she doesn't fit into any conventional pattern."

"How did you get mixed up with this Giorno girl, anyway?" Larry asked.

"She sells notions at Wilkes's store, where I work. We got acquainted and I went out to her house one evening to see some of her drawings."

Jinny curled one leg under her and turned in the seat so that she could watch Larry as she talked. If only she could make him understand. "You should have seen her that night! She's so used to having people disapprove of her that she expects them to, even when they're willing to make friends. I had a hard time winning her confidence."

Larry cocked a knowing eyebrow at her. "You wouldn't be Jinny Somerset if you weren't out championing lost causes half the time. It's a good thing there's somebody around like me to keep you out of trouble."

Jinny went on, ignoring his teasing. "It was all I could do to get her to show me her work. She was so sure I was going to laugh, the way other people have laughed. And when I didn't she kept showing me more and more. Dozens of things she's never shown anyone."

"As freakish as this storm picture?" Larry asked.

"Worse," Jinny said. "But that's not the point. The important thing is Bonita herself, and what's going to happen to her if no one will give her a chance."

There was no time to go on, for Larry had drawn up beside the ramshackle Giorno house.

"You're coming in with me," Jinny told him, and they got out of the car and went up the steps together.

Bonita's mother came to the door, and when she saw the picture Larry carried she shook her head doubtfully. "Bonita didn't want you to take it in the first place. She said nobody would ever want one of her pictures to be shown."

[F.] "Where is she?" Jinny asked, and when Mrs. Giorno nodded toward the rear of the house, she led the way to the back porch.

Bonita was curled up in a creaking swing, her untamed black curls spread against a striped pillow. She wore a yellow blouse and green slacks, and her dark, vivid coloring made one feel there ought to be gold gypsy hoops in her ears. A book lay propped against her raised knees and she munched an apple as she read.

"Hello," Jinny said. "Bonita, this is Larry Bendock who organized the League. I've been telling him about you."

The girl in the swing sat up and gave Larry a brief, defiant look. Then she saw the picture he carried.

"So it wasn't good enough?" she said.

"I thought it was good," Jinny began, but Bonita seemed not to hear her.

"You didn't like it, did you?" she demanded directly of Larry.

"No," he said, "I didn't."

Jinny held her breath. She often had the feeling of being

near an active volcano when she was with Bonita. But after staring at Larry with dark antagonism for a moment, the girl hurled her apple core toward the alley with a vigorous swing of her brown arm. Then she stood up and faced her visitors, arms folded and chin up.

"That's okay," she said. "You wouldn't have liked the storm in Conrad's story, either. Have you ever experienced a typhoon?"

Larry looked startled. "Why, no! Have *you* ever been in one?"

She nodded her black head gravely. "I was in one when I was reading that book. Conrad's a great writer. He made me feel what that storm was like—and I tried to put that feeling on paper. That's what I like to paint—how I feel inside about exciting things. I hate to paint bottles and vases and baskets of fruit. What do I care about this technique they're talking about all the time? I want to paint something that's *happening,* something I can feel, and some day I'll make other people feel those things, too."

"I believe you will," Larry told her soberly. "But just the same, you're taking it the hard way."

When they were back in the car, Jinny turned to him eagerly. "Now do you see why I want to help her? I don't care how many things are wrong with that painting by artistic standards. It has something that most artists never get into their work. And it wasn't copied after all the other storms that have been painted, either. It came out of something that was Joseph Conrad and Bonita Giorno."

"Mm," said Larry noncommittally. "But technique's pretty important to an artist."

"Of course, it's important," Jinny cried, "but it can be learned. What Bonita has in her heart and in her mind can't ever be learned. It's there to begin with, or it isn't there. And not you, nor I, nor anyone else has the right to try to squash it out of her, just because her work doesn't measure up to our kind of standards."

Larry whistled. "If ever I get into a jam, I hope I have you to plug for me!"

"Drop me off at home," she said, and then put a pleading hand on his arm. "Larry, go back and get that picture. There's still time to cast your vote for it and have it hung."

[G.] They drove a block in silence before he answered. "All right," he said at last. "But this is on your head. Something tells me it's going to do Bonita more harm than good to have that picture entered in the exhibit."

[H.] Later that night, when Jinny was home in her own room, she leaned her arms on the window sill and looked out into the moon-shadowed street. She felt all mixed up inside. Perhaps she was wrong, after all, and Larry and the others were right. It was so hard to know. Sometimes she wished rebelliously that she could get old right away. At least as old as thirty, because, obviously, people of thirty knew what it was all about, knew all the things she couldn't know at eighteen.

By the next night, however, she had managed to recover an outward semblance of calm. She was able to meet the famous Burgess Chalmers and talk to him about her own aims as an artist. His line of work—illustrating children's books—was what she wanted to do eventually herself, and there were many questions to ask. But all the time the uneasiness about Bonita's picture was there in her mind, and she couldn't feel quite comfortable.

Larry drove Mr. Chalmers to the library early in the evening, so that he could study the exhibit and make his selections for the prize awards. Jinny went over with Diane just before the crowd began to arrive.

[I.] She saw the picture at once, and her heart gave a little bump that was both elation and apprehension. Down toward one corner of the room the order of the paintings had been rearranged. Place had been made for one more, and there, next to a charming and vacuous still life, hung Bonita Giorno's lurid *Storm*. The gilt frame had been removed and one of natural wood substituted. It looked much better in the new frame, but it still wasn't Art as Poplar City understood it.

Camp chairs had been lined up the length of the room, and Jinny played usher busily for a half hour before everybody was settled. Then she joined Larry and Diane at the speaker's table, where the committee was to reign.

Diane had discovered the picture and was obviously annoyed. She nudged Jinny as she sat down.

"You talked Larry into it, didn't you? And now we're all going to look like fools before the evening is over. How *could* you do a thing like that?"

There was no use in trying to defend her action. Larry was about to introduce Mr. Chalmers, so Jinny said, "Sh-sh," and sat back in her chair.

Later she found herself unable to remember either the details of Larry's introduction, or the gems of wisdom given out by Burgess Chalmers in the course of his talk. Because just at the moment when Mr. Chalmers got up to speak, her roving eyes discovered Bonita Giorno's curly black head in the back row.

She spent the rest of the evening going hot and cold. This

whole thing was her doing and the outcome was on her shoulders. She was alternately terrified at what might lie ahead and elated because she'd managed to get a picture of Bonita's into the exhibit.

[J.] Burgess Chalmers was an excellent speaker and he held his audience, with the possible exception of Jinny, to the end. He looked the successful artist, with his thick white hair, white Van Dyke beard, and bright blue eyes that seemed to miss nothing in the room.

He gave the three small awards to pictures everyone had known would receive them, and said pleasantly flattering things about the artists. He praised the work the Art League was doing in developing talent and bringing to the fore young artists who might otherwise have to struggle alone, without encouragement.

Jinny realized that his talk was nearly over and that with its ending would come the deluge. She had already noticed curious looks being cast in the direction of Bonita's picture. She glanced sidewise at Larry and caught his eye. He shrugged in a manner that said all too plainly, "You asked for this—and we're going to get it."

"In this connection," Mr. Chalmers went on, and she began suddenly to listen, "I want to comment particularly on the painting by Bonita Giorno, entitled *Storm*. Seldom have I seen a piece of work so clumsily executed. There is something about young Miss Giorno's storm that makes me positively seasick when I look at it."

He beamed genially at the room and everyone laughed. Jinny felt a little seasick herself. She didn't dare look at Bonita.

Mr. Chalmers continued, "Now and then, when I have

been asked to serve as judge at some exhibit, I have found on the walls a picture like this one, showing a dismaying lack of knowledge of an artist's tools—and yet with this same crude power and vitality. I congratulate your committee for having the courage to hang such a picture here."

The room was hushed. Those who had been ready to laugh were no longer sure of Mr. Chalmer's direction.

"If I had the courage of your committee," he continued, "and was not constrained by custom to awarding prizes to the most technically excellent paintings, I would have given first award without hesitation to that picture. It has an originality of idea and conception that sets the artist far ahead of those who know only how to paint correctly. Which does not mean that young Miss Bonita doesn't need to buckle down and learn how to draw, but only that if she is willing to learn, she may quite possibly have a successful career ahead of her."

[K.] Mr. Chalmers sat down amid applause, and Jinny's quick eye saw Bonita slip out at the side door. She leaned over and touched Larry's arm.

"Look! There she goes. We've got to catch her and make her come back to talk to him."

They hurried outside together as the meeting broke up.

"I get it now," Larry admitted when they had Bonita safely between them. "About what you said, I mean. Something of Bonita Giorno and Joseph Conrad."

Jinny nodded. "Some of us were trying to make her just Poplar City," she said, feeling warm and happy inside.

XI

PUTTING IT TOGETHER

In the preceding chapter you will find reprinted a story of mine which appeared in the *American Girl*. I want to use this as a case story because I understand so well the problems which went into the writing of it. I know why certain things were done, and why others had to be done over. But before we go into an analysis of the story, we had better look at the separate parts which make up a story. A plotted story will break naturally into the following sections:

> Opening
> Body
> Climax
> Denouement

Thinking of your story as a series of scenes, you will assign one scene to the opening, possibly a single scene to climax and denouement together, though this is not necessarily a rule, and the remainder of your scenes to the body of the story.

Each of these sections is important and the misuse of any one of them can ruin the effect of your story. The opening, however, is your show window and some of your most careful effort must go into that. You have just one chance to catch the interest of your young reader. That chance lies on your first page. It may even lie in your first paragraph. No matter what exciting things you know are going to happen on page six, your reader (and incidentally the editor) will not stay with you that long unless you sell him on page one the idea of reading more.

There are various methods of beginning a story and your material will to some extent govern this. It is always a wise author, however, who does more governing than being governed when it comes to technique. Whatever your choice of opening methods, remember that your problem should be made clear as soon as possible. That means that it must, first of all, be clear in your own mind. So clear that in your planning process you wrote it down in a sentence or two and will never thereafter forget what *this* story is supposed to be about. It isn't always possible to get the problem stated completely on the first page, but you can weave in direct leads which point to it, so that the reader knows immediately that there *is* a problem and that the main character is trying to do something about it.

There are four ways in which I might have opened the case story. I might have used narration, or exposition. I might have opened with dialogue between two or more characters. I might have presented one character thinking about something. Or I could open with action: one or more characters doing something interesting. I'd like to give a brief example of each method, but I'll go on record as being in favor of the last one only. The other examples are presented merely as how *not* to do it.

If you are writing for young people there are no two ways about it—you open your story in the most interesting manner you can. Narration is never very gripping. Conversation between people you know nothing about is not at all arresting. One character thinking about his problem is pretty dull. But action—one or more characters doing something interesting which happens right before the reader's eyes—ah, there is the hook which will keep him reading.

Remember to consider your audience in working out your story opening. The idea is to present characters in whom he is likely to be interested, doing something which is likely to interest him. If your opening action concerns characters much older, or much younger than he is, he'll turn the page of the magazine to another story. You can count on just one glance at your show window. You catch your reader's interest then, or you probably lose it for good.

Here is an example of a story which opens with narration. (In passing I'd like to say that the "Jinny Somerset" of this *American Girl* story is the same "Ginny Somerset" of *A Star for Ginny* and *A Place for Ann*. The magazine editor preferred to change the spelling and it is always wise to let an editor have her way.)

Jinny Somerset wanted to get into the basement of the library quietly. She knew her friends who were hanging pictures for the Young People's Art League would not approve of the picture she was carrying. It was unfortunate that she should trip on the top step and fall downstairs.

When everyone came out to see what had happened she told them she was not hurt. After Larry Bendock had helped her to her feet she carried the picture into the exhibition room. She told the others that they would have to make room for another picture because this one would have to be hung. Diane Chalmers said she did not think the girl who had painted the picture had very much talent and that she did not want to see it hung.

This, of course, is the author *telling* the reader about it. It is not a scene that you can see and hear. The characters are mere names and you feel nothing whatsoever in reading about them. Narration, exposition, is a practically sure way to kill your reader's interest in the story before he gets to the bottom of the first page. It is often a temptation to the beginner to use that method, because it is the simplest way to make your problem clear. It is a lot more trouble and it takes much longer to weave information into dialogue and direct action than to plunk it down in statements at the opening of the story. Nevertheless, if you want to get your story past a first reading, I suggest that you avoid narration like the pest it is.

Another means, less evil, of opening a story is to use dialogue immediately. An opening of that kind might read like this:

"I'm not hurt," Jinny said quickly as her friends came running out of the library exhibition room to see if she had hurt herself in falling downstairs.

"Don't touch her till she's counted her bones," Larry Bendock warned. "There's no use picking her up if she's going to fall apart on our hands."

"I tell you I'm all right," Jinny said, getting to her feet and picking up the big gilt frame she was carrying. "I hope you have room for one more picture in the exhibit. I had to take this away from Bonita Giorno practically by force."

"Bonita Giorno!" Diane Chalmers echoed. "She hasn't any talent and I don't think people like that should be encouraged."

This is not too bad, but it is still not good enough. Why should a reader care what a person is saying until he knows something about that person? In both these versions the problem is presented quickly, but the manner of presentation is not too interesting.

Here is a third method which shows a character thinking about her problems:

> As Jinny Somerset walked toward the library she wondered how in the world she was going to get Bonita's picture into the exhibit without attracting the attention of the other young people in the Art League. They would be in the basement exhibition room of the library tonight and she knew they would disapprove of Bonita's picture. She recalled Bonita's hesitation about allowing her to take the picture and . . .

This could go on for some wordage and I'm sure no one would care. The thoughts of your viewpoint character are going to come into your story again and again, but they do not make interesting reading until the reader is well acquainted with the character and knows what he is trying to do.

Far better to present some plausible characters who immediately conflict because of something the main character wants to accomplish. Then the reader can give his allegiance, and once having done so will want to see his side win. When you must of necessity open with just one character on the scene, show him doing something interesting before you allow him to think about it. But your task will be simplified if you can have another character, or even an animal, present for him to talk to.

"Storm Over the Art League" opens with the method most writers have tried and found true. It opens with *something happening*. The first paragraph is direct action. In this case it happens to be exciting action and no reader is likely to stop there. A tumble downstairs is an experience anyone can sympathize with; the reader's attention is arrested and she will want to know what happens next.

The second paragraph is narration. Here the writer tells you what happened, but presents the necessary information in words which leave a picture in the reader's mind. Having been caught by dramatic action in the first paragraph, she is willing to stay with the story through a paragraph of explanation, providing it is brief. In paragraph three we return to direct action, and in the next paragraph swing into dialogue.

The problem is not made clear so quickly this time as in the other two versions, but interest is caught. At point "A" a problem comes into the story. It is not *the* problem, though it leads directly to it. Jinny's main problem in the story is to win recognition of Bonita Giorno's talent. However, this does not become clear until the second scene. In the opening her immediate problem is to sneak the picture unseen into the library. A problem which meets with defeat because of her fall downstairs and arouses curiosity in the reader's mind. Why is she trying to sneak the picture into the library? What will she do about it now that she has failed?

Every scene must leave the reader asking one or more questions. The moment her curiosity is satisfied she is going to put the story down and I, as story-teller, will be through. The technique of suspense consists in keeping the curiosity of the reader aroused until the very last page and then satisfying it completely. Thus there must be, not only a main story problem which ties everything together, but a number of contributing problems as well, one or more to each succeeding scene. These may meet with either success or failure. Failure in itself carries the reader on to see what the character will do next (as in the opening of this story). Success can put a period to interest, unless more problems and obstacles appear the moment one is solved.

At point "B" the opening scene has come to an end. It is not necessary, of course, to pattern *your* opening exactly after that of any written story. This is not a mathematical matter and what you do with your opening will depend on your individual material, but there are certain matters it is wise to accomplish in that opening scene.

Start with something happening to one or more of your characters. This doesn't always mean action as dramatic as a fall downstairs. It does, however, imply action that means something to your story. Never *meaningless* action.

In my first writing of this story the action with which it opened was completely meaningless. It was a trick opening to hook reader interest in a story I found difficult to present at once in dramatic form. Jinny was not trying for secrecy the first time, but simply fell noisily downstairs in order to interest my reader. Tricks are unfair and apt to lose their effect the moment the reader discovers that the cry of "Fire!" was a false alarm. So the opening was reworked and the element of secrecy inserted. If it is important to Jinny to get that picture quietly into the library, then her fall downstairs defeats that purpose and really has something to do with the story.

Having opened with something happening, keep your exposition as brief as possible and avoid it altogether if you can. Get into dialogue quickly. Once your reader has been introduced to people who are doing something, he wants to hear them talk. Get your important characters into the story as early as possible. In this story four characters are of major importance: Jinny, Larry, Bonita, and Diane. Jinny and Larry are introduced at once, and a glimpse is given of Diane on her stepladder. In each case there is an indication of what sort of person each character is and a glimpse is given of that character's appearance. It is not possible to bring Bonita on the scene until later in the story, but her name is mentioned early in the story and by the second scene the reader is made aware that the problem concerns her.

If possible, avoid the use of flashback in your story. It *can* be used skillfully and effectively, but its dangers are many and editors will like you better if you avoid it. If a flashback scene is very important, it may be wiser to start with that scene, presenting it in direct action, instead of as something which happened before the start of your story. Then, by means of well-handled transition, you can connect it to the later scenes and get on with the story.

The danger of the flashback lies in the loss of reader interest at each break. If I had started my story with Jinny falling downstairs and then carried it back to an earlier scene in which Jinny talked to Bonita and persuaded her to allow the picture to be submitted, there would have been a break in interest when I left the library scene. Then, even if I handled the flashback between Jinny and Bonita effectively, there would be a second let-down when I returned to the present. Reader interest is a prize to be treated tenderly. It is better not to run the risk of inflicting extra interest-breaks upon him; you may have trouble enough holding him to your story as it is.

In this instance I wove the information necessary to the story into the words of the characters, so that no flashback was necessary. The time element was held to a minimum. The story starts on one evening and ends the next.

Your opening scenes may be longer or shorter than this one of mine—there is no law concerning that. But the ingredients I have listed should go into that opening.

Point "C" is a transition scene. Get your characters from one place to another with as much dispatch as possible. It is never necessary to tell every move they make at these places in your action. The important thing is to get the curtain raised on the next scene as quickly as you can.

At the end of point "C" we have the next story scene, this time in the basement room of the library and we are now on our way into the body of the story. We find out why Jinny wanted to sneak the picture in and at point "D" the problem is made evident. Jinny wants to see a picture of Bonita's included in the exhibit.

If at this point, everyone gave in readily, the story would end. There must be *opposition to the problem*. Thus it is made evident at once that Diane is not inclined to be friendly toward Bonita. Through characterization reader-sympathy is thrown with Jinny and Bonita, and against Diane. The reader takes sides.

In plotting this story I had one particular difficulty to circumvent because I was breaking a rule. The problem *should* be the problem of the main character. But as I saw the story in its early form, the problem was far more Bonita's than it was Jinny's. Yet it could not be told as effectively from Bonita's viewpoint. There was the danger of having my main character a bystander whose own interest was not seriously tied in with the problem. To get around this I built up a touch of rivalry between Diane and Jinny for Larry's interest, and put the responsibility for what happened to Bonita and her picture completely on Jinny's shoulders. That made it *her* problem and helped to enlist the sympathies of the reader on her side.

The problem which arises in the second scene is to get the committee of three to vote for the hanging of Bonita's picture. Jinny is on the committee and can cast a vote for it. Diane is sure to vote against it, so the success of Jinny's project hangs on Larry. Suspense is built up by keeping the picture itself hidden from view as long as possible.

If, when the picture is shown, Larry votes for it, the story is over. So again Jinny's purpose must meet with defeat. Larry refuses to see in the picture what Jinny sees and decides against it. But your heroine (or mine) must never give up along the way, so Jinny plays another card which carries the problem over to the next scene and becomes this time an effort to change Larry's mind.

Point "E" is a quick transition scene, with no time wasted getting from the library to Larry's car. Then follows a short scene in the car. During this scene nothing very exciting happens, yet the importance of the problem is built up. (Remember—what depends on your problem? What disaster will come to pass if your protagonist does not succeed in what he is trying to accomplish? What good will be brought about if he succeeds?) This is a "let-down" scene and for a few paragraphs slows the tempo of the story—something that is all to the good. Even in an exciting adventure story it is not wise to wear the reader out with an oversupply of thrills. Break off now and then for a breathing space. Interest is variable. It cannot remain too long at one pitch. An occasional reflective pause during which the characters think about what has happened and what is still to happen, rests the reader and enables him to go on to the next scene with quickened interest. However, even though this scene is an interlude in the story action, it does not permit the story to come to a dead stop. Larry and Jinny are in motion going somewhere. What is to occur in the next scene is of interest to the reader and she will keep reading to find out what happens when they arrive at Bonita's.

There is further transition at point "F" and the next scene takes place when they come upon Bonita in the swing on her porch. Now the problem of convincing Larry that he must help Bonita is further hindered by Bonita herself. She has been badly treated and is resentful and suspicious, but her remark about the typhoon at the end of the scene keeps reader sympathy on her side.

In this scene a story theme begins to inject itself and add significance. Bonita wants to dispense with the bother of learning about technique in her art work. She wants to *do* at once, without the troublesome bother of learning how to do. The theme might be stated as follows: "While it does not do to crush originality and stamp everyone into the same pattern, every workman must learn to use his tools before he can do worthwhile work."

There is another quick transition consisting of one sentence: "When they were back in the car, Jinny turned to him eagerly . . ." and we are into another brief scene in the car as Larry drives Jinny home.

An important fact to note about these changing scenes is that every scene grows out of the action which took place in the scene before, and in turn gives rise to the action which follows in the next scene. If at any place along the line you find yourself with a scene on your hands which does not grow directly out of a previous scene and move directly into the next one, you had better discard it entirely. No matter how filled it is with delightful incident in its own right, no matter how much of your best work has gone into it, if it is not tied to the main stem of your story plan, you will have to put it aside. Of course, if you planned carefully in the beginning, no such scenes will pop unexpectedly into being during the writing of your story.

Again Jinny's immediate problem is to convince Larry that Bonita's picture should be hung in the exhibit. At the end of this short scene she has rung a reluctant promise from him. Again there could be a let-down of interest in the solving of this particular problem, unless some threat to success is immediately raised. This is done through Larry's foreboding remarks at point "G." The paragraph at "H" is a reflective pause which gives Jinny time to do a little worrying and summing up.

Through two transition paragraphs which present necessary information, we get Jinny to the library and into the following evening by point "I" (transitions may be of both time and space, or of either one). Now we are moving on toward the climax scene. In this case, the early part of the scene is presented with touches of direct action and quite a bit of exposition. If all of this scene were presented in direct action it would be filled with unimportant detail which would take too long and would hold up the movement of the story. By now the reader wants to know what is going to happen and will be willing to read through a moderate amount of exposition in order to get to the point of interest. However, even though some of this is narration, it is still given through Jinny's eyes and suspense is being built up. The main story problem is in complete evidence now. Can Jinny succeed in winning for Bonita the recognition she feels the girl deserves?

The obstacles mount and disaster threatens. Bonita's picture, though hung in the exhibit, is still obviously not art as Poplar City understands it. Diane intimates that thanks to Jinny, the art committee will look like fools before the evening is over. Jinny discovers that Bonita is present at the affair. Defeat will further injure her and it will be Jinny's fault. Will everything Jinny has tried to do result in calamity?

This is the black moment just before dawn. If you can bring your story to the very brink of disaster at this point, the reader's satisfaction with your happy ending will be all the more keen. In the planning of this story a serious problem came up at this point. The best way to end a story is to give it a twist in a direction the reader did not expect. In this case the reader has been made to feel that it would be illogical for Bonita to win the prize, and yet, being conditioned to happy endings, she probably expects her to win it. If I had fulfilled that hope and given the reader exactly what she expected, I might have had to throw logic to the winds, and in following the accustomed path would have made the story ending less satisfying. At this point in the planning I began to seek for a twist the reader would not expect. What if I gave the awards to other contestants? That would take the story along an unexpected road, but at the same time it would leave the reader with the bad taste of an unsatisfying ending. I had to figure out a way in which to defeat Bonita and Jinny and yet give them a better reward than any small prize could be—defeat turned into success. In order to accomplish this sort of story ending, you carry your heroine to the brink of disaster and then actually have disaster befall her. At this point the reader will ring her hands mentally and protest that there is no way out. And there is not a chance in the world that she will stop reading at that point. In conclusion you perform your sleight-of-hand and end everything happily in spite of disaster.

At "J" the real climax begins. This is the place in the story where the writer must deliver the goods. It is for this emotional satisfaction that the reader has read through earlier scenes. Fail him at this point and your story goes quickly back home accompanied by a rejection slip. Yet how often have I seen young writers build up good stories, carry them to the climax scene and then, overcome by self-consciousness, stage-fright, paralysis, or laziness, skip the whole scene! Then we have a denouement in which the protagonist congratulates himself upon solving his problem and perhaps recalls in retrospect some of the details of the climax scene.

Please don't be guilty of that. The climax scene may be brief, but wring every bit of drama you can out of it. Play it big and bring down the house with applause. Don't muff it, don't ring down the curtain in the middle of the scene and leave your reader with a flat taste of disappointment.

I attempted to carry my suspense to the very last moment by having Mr. Chalmer's remarks throw further gloom upon Jinny's hopes. Then in his final words he gives Bonita high praise, yet points up the theme by telling her she must still buckle down and learn to use the tools of her trade. A theme which has significance for other readers besides artists (if there are any writers present, I *do* mean you).

When Mr. Chalmers sits down ("K") the story is over. The reader's curiosity has been satisfied. However, there are usually a few threads to be tied at this point and a denouement scene must follow to conclude the story. This should be as brief as possible because now you have really lost your reader's interest and must be willing to let it go. Tie your bow neatly and let him get away in no more than a few paragraphs. The one rule for this scene is to recognize when your story is over (some writers never seem to know) and come to a quick conclusion.

If you like, you can check this story against the questions listed in Chapter V and see how many of them can be answered in the affirmative.

We cannot talk about putting a story together without some comment concerning style. Very often the young writer feels that style is something he must strive for by much polishing, by a studious choice of words, by various "literary" touches. It is true that most manuscripts can stand polishing, and that choice of words is important. But forget about being literary. Forget about impressing anyone with fine writing. Children are not interested in style. They are interested in *story*.

Aim for clarity, no matter what age you write for, and style need cause you no concern. It is a matter which will develop by itself and be individual with you when you have put enough writing hours behind you.

Word books have been of great use to me. My *Roget's Thesaurus* has rescued me many times and aided me in making sure of the right word. No matter how excellent your vocabulary, it is not a good *working* vocabulary unless words come easily to mind when you want them. I believe the years I spent using these books has improved my working vocabulary. I seldom need to refer to word books now, because my own word reservoir is well filled. Again, this is a matter of habit and training. Keep one of these books handy on your desk and reach for it the moment you are stumped.

In the final reckoning the proof of your story pudding lies in presentation. The most excellent framework in the world can be spoiled by poor presentation. And sometimes very slipshod plots get by on presentation alone. Presentation does not mean style. It means how well you bring your characters alive, how cleverly you snare the reader's interest, how successful you are in achieving the illusion of reality. In short, how skillfully you use all the cutting blades of that many-edged tool—technique.

The final writing of your story may prove difficult as you first try to apply the tool of technique. You will remember one thing, only to forget another. You may despair of ever getting everything right at the same time; or even of getting a moderate number of things right at the same time, which is the best most of us can hope for. You will undoubtedly discover that whatever ease of writing you may have known has taken leave of you and that you are now awkward and self-conscious. Don't let this disturb you. Revision will straighten out many of the things that are wrong, and as you write more and more stories, the ease will come.

In my planning period I think a great deal about technique, but in the actual writing I have learned to think of it not at all. Practice in using any tool will enable you at last to use it without considering the tool itself and then you will begin to get results. If you allow yourself to despair before that ease comes, you will have only yourself to blame if you fall by the way.

XII

TAKING IT APART

"But I *can't* rewrite. Everything is fresh the first time. When I try to do it over, it takes all the life out of the story."

How many times I've heard novices say that! How many times I said it myself when I was a beginner! Again it's that subconscious imp talking. He doesn't care about your story, or whether there is any life in it or not. What he does care about is not having the life taken out of him by further odious work. After all, he has helped you write the story, hasn't he? If it weren't for him you'd still be looking at a blank sheet of paper. So why can't you be satisfied and leave him in peace?

But he knows you'll do nothing of the kind unless he makes his plea sound logical and rational. So he whispers that you mustn't think of touching your little masterpiece. It is alive and sparkling now, even though unintelligent and unsympathetic critics may see a few chips around the edges. Better, far better, to overlook those chipped places than to take the sparkle out of the jewel.

Unfortunately, the editor will see those chips immediately and back will come your story—which probably never should have been sent off in the first place. You might as well face the facts right now. It will undoubtedly take the life out of *you*, the writer, to do it over, but it is not likely to take it out of the story.

Of course what is needed is not aimless revision; revision without benefit of direction or guidance. You must know what to look for. Again I suggest that you use the check list in Chapter V and apply it carefully to your completed story. If you are not sure of all the answers—as it is very likely you will not be, since no writer is an absolutely satisfactory judge of his own work—then seek out some competent critic who will see the story more clearly than you do and will be able to point out its weaknesses.

It is wiser not to revise immediately. When you reach the last page and write THE END, you are apt to experience a deceptive glow. If you sit down and read that story over then you will probably be entranced with its virtues. You are very close to it, you have an affection for it, and one does not see with a sufficiently jaundiced eye through the rosy hazes of first love.

Of course you will want to send your darling off in the mail at once so that you can get a check back from the editor post-haste, but I suggest that you control this impulse and put the story away to "set."

Remember—it's the story that is to "set," not yourself. *You* are going to get busy immediately on a new story. When you have given your fickle affections to a new love, you will be in a far better position to go back and look at the old love with a critical eye.

When I was writing short stories regularly, I worked out a system. I always tried to keep at least two stories "on ice" that had as yet not gone into the mail. When I finished a third one, I put that on the bottom of the stack and took out the top one for a rereading. By that time the rosy haze had been dispelled and I could regard the story with anything but pleasure. A hearty disliking is probably the only healthy attitude to be entertained toward any story that has not seen print. After that story is in print and nothing further can be done to it, you may again be permitted a fatuous affection for it. Until that time, look only for its faults. Don't worry—they are there.

Above all, don't corner some unfortunate friend who knows nothing about writing and read it aloud to him. If he likes you, he'll probably like your story, whether it is any good or not. Just because your friends may read does not necessarily qualify them as critics.

This is where that writing circle comes in, if you belong to one. Read it to them and you'll probably receive some healthy dashes of cold water, unless your group pulls its punches and goes in for polite pats on the back—in which case it might as well disband for all the good it will do any of you.

The best thing of all is to have somewhere in your life a really competent critic. If you find one whose judgment you can trust, treat him tenderly, guard him gently, for his worth is beyond price. Don't argue with him and tell him he's all wrong and that he simply hasn't the sensitivity to understand this delicate thing you are trying to accomplish in your story. Say "Yes, sir," meekly and go home and think about what he has told you. Then get busy and rewrite your story.

Oh, of course, *you* are different. You can take criticism. You understand perfectly that nothing personal is implied. If your critic says your hero is a bit on the stupid side, it doesn't mean that *you* are stupid. You are not going to be upset in any way by what is said. You are asking for help because you really want it and you desire to make this story as perfect as you possibly can.

Don't fool yourself. You don't really mean a word of it. What you do mean is that you feel quite safe in asking for criticism because you know how good your story is and you are sure no one is going to say anything against it. What you really want is oil for your vanity, praise for your brain child, incense for your altar.

When the critic rips your story limb from limb and leaves it a heap of rubble, the shock is going to send you into a state of collapse. You are not going to listen to a word of it with your mind—you are going to take the whole thing full force with your emotions. You are going to be crushed, wounded, left bleeding and despairing. All your high hopes have died, your dreams have been dispelled. How *could* this person whom you so trusted prove to be such a brute and do you so much injury? Why, now you don't even feel like writing any more. Your career has been blasted. You'll show him what he's done to you. Then he'll feel sorry.

He won't. He'll merely look at you coldly, dust off his hands and walk away. And next time he'll know better. Next time when you go to him for help (as you undoubtedly will) he'll regard you sadly and shake his head. After all, he has his own sensitivities, and he'd rather keep you as a friend (goodness knows why!) than so alienate you with his criticism of your story.

You may, if you like, disregard everything else I've told you in this book, but listen to me, please, on this. Good stories are not written. They are *re*written.

So you will have to set about growing callouses in the right places. Emotion is something which has a very definite place in your story, but it has no place at all in the way in which you receive criticism. Take it for granted that there will be plenty wrong with your story. Perfection is all too rare. Most stories which get published have plenty wrong with them and could be improved still further. See to it that revision improves your story to the limit of your ability before you send it out. Listen to your critics *with your mind,* weigh and consider and never, never argue. If in the final judgment you disagree, that is your affair. But don't wrangle over anything they tell you. Store it away and consider it soberly.

Revision is an unpleasant, grubby job. It is a dull, boring, hateful job. But it is perhaps the most important part of writing. Revision certainly takes the life out of a writer. All the freshness, all the adventure, all the excitement of meeting new characters is gone and you may have the greatest loathing for every word you set down during revision. Oddly enough, your own feeling on the matter does not seem to show in the final version. The passages which were written with sweat and blood and hatred very often sound much better than those allowed to stand as they were first written.

One of the reasons I have used "Storm Over the Art League" as a case story is because of the revision that went into it. At the time when I wrote it I belonged to a seminar class directed by Frederic Nelson Litten. The story was read aloud and each member of the group gave his impressions. The first verdict was a thorough thumbs down. I stuffed my broken heart into my handbag and made careful notes on all the criticism offered.

It was pointed out that Jinny's fall downstairs in the opening paragraph was meaningless action. In revising I gave her a motive for sneaking the picture into the library and made the fall the defeat of her first effort. In the first version I had her fall down a flight of five steps and the comment was made that she would probably have broken her neck. The steps were changed to three and Jinny announces immediately that she is unhurt. As it read the first time, Larry's remarks sounded callous and unsympathetic, since it wasn't made clear quickly that she was unhurt.

There was no Bonita in the first version. Instead, I had a boy named Mike. This caused confusion as to hero interest. Was Jinny to be interested in Larry, or in the boy she was befriending? When this was pointed out I immediately saw the advantage of making the artist a girl, and worked out the character, Bonita Giorno.

Bonita later proved unexpectedly useful to me. Girls who read the story were interested in her and several suggested that I write more about her. I was working on the plan for *A Window for Julie* at the time and saw the need for just such a character as Bonita for the book. So Bonita, who grew out of revision, took her place in opposition to my heroine, Julie.

In the first version, Mike was not only the wrong sex for the part, but he was sullen and unsympathetic, too. Here is a speech he made in the original story when Jinny brings the picture back and tells him it won't be hung:

> "That's okay," said Mike stiffly. "I didn't want to send it over anyway. I know I'm no good. I can't paint pretty flowers and cute kids, or any of that other stuff you'll hang in the exhibit. I only had a feeling about the storm in that story, and I wanted to put that feel-

ing on paper. But it wouldn't come out like I had it in my mind. I should have torn it up when I was through. I don't know anything about painting."

The criticism was made that Mike was so unpleasant no reader would understand why Jinny wanted to help him. Contrast this speech with the one Bonita makes in the printed version.

In the first attempt I fell into an error which I certainly knew enough to avoid. My heroine did nothing herself to solve the problem. She simply stood around being angry and indignant. In fact, Jinny herself was not too sympathetic a character the first time. In rewriting she sets out deliberately to persuade Larry to hang the picture. It is through her effort that Bonita gets her chance. Changing her from an unsympathetic character to a more pleasant one was a simple matter. I went through the manuscript and substituted words and phrases wherever this sort of thing appeared: "said crossly," "snapped," "hanging onto her already ruffled temper," "Jinny repeated stubbornly."

In the first story, when the hanging of the painting is voted down, there was this passage:

> Jinny said, "I'd never expected to see Larry Bendock turn into an artistic snob," and picked up the picture with as much dignity as she could muster, considering that she had to struggle to carry it at all.
>
> There were angry tears stinging her eyelids, but she walked the length of the big room with her nose in the air, and went out into the warm evening. It was blocks across the tracks to Mike's house, but there was nothing to do but lug the picture back to its creator.
>
> She paid no attention when a car pulled up beside her

and a raucous horn was blown. Larry had to get out and catch up with her on foot. He took the picture from under her arm without ceremony.

"Nobody gets away with calling *me* an artistic snob," he said. "Get in the car and I'll drive you over to Mike's. You can explain yourself on the way."

This made for unsympathetic treatment in the case of both Jinny and Larry. Often in writing for young people it is necessary to have a character who is mistaken in behavior and learns a better way by the end of the story. But this sort of thing must be carefully handled and a delicate balance kept or the reader will be thrown thoroughly out of sympathy with your main character, so that he won't care whether that character solves his problem or not. In this case, my mistaken character was Bonita, not Jinny, so there was no excuse for making Jinny behave badly. Besides, when she was behaving badly, she merely walked out and everything "happened" through no effort of hers. In a story nothing must "just happen." It must be *made* to happen through the efforts of your main character. Compare the scene as it was published with the above. In the second version nobody gets mad and Jinny has a real plan to make Larry understand the situation.

In the first story, after their visit to the artist, Jinny parts from Larry like this:

She was so mad she wouldn't talk to him any more, and when he pulled up before her house, she got out and slammed the car door rudely behind her.

In the second effort it is handled this way:

"Drop me off at home," she said, and then put a pleading hand on his arm. "Larry, go back and get that picture. There's still time to cast your vote for it and have it hung."

Very little was done to the climax in rewriting, except to exchange Mike for Bonita. But the denouement was preachy and without real justification the first time, so I deleted a good part of it. I am still not satisfied with the last paragraphs in the published version. The conclusion is abrupt and not as smooth as it should have been. Which means that I should have carried my revision still further.

Every writer has a blind spot concerning his own work. It *is* possible to develop through constant practice on your own stories, and those of your writing friends, a keenly critical attitude. But you will never see everything yourself. That is why it is a great help to have a competent critic or two in the offing. Lacking an outside critic to point out mistakes, a writer is likely enough to go on making the same ones over and over without being aware of them.

However, before you take your story to a critic, see what you can do with some revision of your own. Check it against all the things you were supposed to accomplish in the original planning.

1. Is the problem clear? Is it one which will interest the age for which your story is intended?

2. Are your characters individualized? Are they consistent? Are the main character and his problem presented sympathetically?

3. What point are you trying to make, and did you make it?

4. Is there a subsidiary problem in every scene, and a carry-over of interest to the next scene?

5. Is there a scene which could be lifted bodily from the story without having it missed?

6. Is your climax emotionally satisfying?

7. What about logic and motivation? Do these ring true, or were you trying to force some action to suit your own purposes?

These last two are especially important. If you have portrayed your leading character in a certain way, there are some things it would be illogical to have him do. He must stay *in character* all the way through. His every move must be properly motivated.

Learn to listen to the inner voice which will whisper to you and question certain matters in your story. Often it is not a very insistent voice and you may brush it aside because you want to think everything is all right and you can "get by" on this score. I have learned that if there is so much as a hint of doubt from that voice, I'd better check into the matter thoroughly and do a little revision at that point. Otherwise, I usually find to my regret that this is the very angle some critic leaps gleefully upon and rips to shreds.

There is no easy road to getting a story right. But in the long run you will find that grubbing at this point pays.

XIII

Specialization

It is quite likely that after you have experimented for a while with the writing of various types of stories, you will want to narrow the field down and specialize in some one or two particular types. You will decide whether you want to write for boys or girls, whether you want to write about the modern scene or use historical material, whether you want to write for the teens, the in-between age, or for younger children. In these groups there may be still further specialization.

Your best guide, when you decide upon some special field is to go to the children's room of any library and stock up on books in that field. Read them in quantity until you know them well enough to compare the merits of different writers, and to recognize their flaws. Do this whether you intend to write books or not. Talk to children's librarians and find out what the youngsters themselves think. Why do the books of one author get worn to the replacing stage in a comparatively short period, while the books of another sit untouched on the shelves? You can find out these things best by doing some research of your own, and by reading books written for the age you have selected. Steep yourself in what is being written in that field. That way you can learn, too, what has been done over and over so many times that you had better avoid it. You can discover where you can contribute a fresh slant. This, of course, goes for the magazine field as well. Read copies of the magazines for which you want to write so that you will know what each editor is buying.

In this chapter we will take a brief glance at a few special fields. All I can do is point out some possibilities and issue a few warnings.

FANTASY

If you intend to write for young children it is very possible that you will be attracted first of all to the idea of writing about make-believe. The advice I must give you at this point can be put in one word: "Don't!"

It isn't that children do not care for stories of make-believe. Most children love them. And it isn't that editors are not delighted to print really good stories of this kind. The difficulty lies in the fact that fantasy is the easiest thing of all to write badly, and the most difficult to do well.

Editors' desks are piled high with tales of "Little Miss Moonbeam," or "The Unhappy Pumpkin Seed," or "The Little Lost Cloud." The chances are good that if you write that sort of thing you won't be read past the first page. In fact, the editor will probably pull your story halfway out of its envelope, say, "Oh, another one!" and send it straight back. If you are trying to break in, I assure you, fantasy is no Open Sesame. You need unusual talent, wisdom, a wonderful sense of humor, and an expert way with words before you can turn out something outstanding in this field, and even then the chances are against your selling it. This is because the editor in turn also has trouble selling fantasy, and all editors are in business to sell books.

This brings us to the bookstore—where fantasy meets its major defeat. Clerks in bookstores know how hard it is to sell stories of make-believe to customers unless they are titles already familiar to the buyer.

Recently I heard a writer who was also a father bemoaning the fact that fantasy is so hard to sell these days. "My little girl loves it," he told me. "So why don't the fantasies I write get published? I asked him what sort of fantasy (besides his own) he read to his daughter and he had all the titles ready: *Wind in the Willows, Mary Poppins, Alice in Wonderland, The Wizard of Oz, Winnie the Pooh*—and so on. All the classics. And this is exactly the reason why *new* fantasy is so difficult to get published. The people who go into a bookstore to purchase books for children refuse to adventure when it comes to fantasy. They are willing to accept the bookseller's advice on modern, realistic stories, but they know all about fantasy, thank you, and they will have only what they read as children.

From time to time there is a resurgence of interest in fantasy, and new stories do get published. But they have to be very good indeed because they must compete with genius.

If you must write fantasy, it is a good rule to avoid stories about inanimate objects. It is very difficult to give a seashell a sense of emotion, and if you are to retain some feeling of reality, the inanimate object must remain stationary unless it is carried from place to place by something that can move. Beware particularly of having the inanimate smile, frown, laugh, wink, etc. Though you'll see this happen sometimes in the story for the very young, where the artist is able to give the little automobile, or whatever, an amusing face. If you must write about the inanimate, then some object close to a child makes a better choice, such as a teddy bear, or a doll. But you'll need to come up with something original.

So—if you *must* write fantasy, try to do it in the modern way. Leave out the fairies and witches and elves, and imaginary kingdoms like Oz. Let your fantasy happen in today's world, among everyday events. This type of make-believe stands a better chance of selling than the old-fashioned kind. Your librarian should be able to show you good examples of modern stories of the imagination.

Remember, however, that these stories are not for children over eight as far as our age categories go. Fantasy for young people in their teens is almost impossible to sell, no matter how much some individual teen-agers might enjoy it. The exception is science fiction, which is perhaps today's version of the fairy story and allows the young reader the same stretching of the imagination.

ANIMAL STORIES

These are often kin to fantasy, but you are on safer ground. Animal stories are perennial favorites with young people of all ages. The convention observed in this field seems to be that if your animals talk, they should talk only among themselves and not to the human beings in the story. This rule, however, is broken successfully a good many times during every publishing year, so I don't want to be arbitrary about it.

Stories of make-believe often seem to be more acceptable when they deal with animals than when they deal with people. Though of course any mixture of the two is possible.

In writing animal fantasy, certain creatures lend themselves less readily to the effective story. You'd better not write about fish, turtles, snails or snakes. Even a bird in a cage is difficult to write about. Beginners are always trying these with little success. Something more lovable and cuddly, with more evident emotions of its own, makes a better choice. Parakeet lovers need not write me indignant letters. A parakeet is hard to write about unless used as a realistic part of a story about children.

The most popular animal story today is the one about real animals living as animals do, whether they be wild or tame. Alice Goudey and Robert McClung have done outstanding examples of this type of book.

Pets are, of course, useful in any sort of story and can often help your plot along to a great degree. Don't forget them in writing stories for children.

The educational factor enters here to the writer's advantage. If you know a great deal about the habits of some particular animal, stories about him will probably be welcome. You may even become another Felix Salten and give the world a *Bambi*.

HISTORICAL

If you have a natural flair for writing of the past, this is a good field to specialize in. You may write about any period or phase of history you like—all time and the entire world is yours to choose from. But first you must steep yourself in the land and period until you feel as if you had lived in that place and time yourself.

From the picture-book age to the teens, the historical is regarded with a kindly eye by editors and librarians. These stories are sure to be "educational" and often, sad to relate, this point weighs so heavily in their favor that much that is rather dull gets published and inflicted upon young readers.

One of the "tricks" of writing this type of story is to make your young people sound very much as they do today. Get the flavor of the time into your dialogue, but avoid stiffness and formality. Don't make the characters speak exactly in the words they might have used at that time in history. Though of course you must avoid any use of current slang or the result will jar. Get to know your characters as if they were youngsters who live on your block, rather than distant figures who belong in the past. They must be made very real and sympathetic to young people today. The more strange and foreign the names of your people may be, the better must your characterization be. It is very easy to imagine a girl named Mary because we have all known so many Marys, both in fiction and in life. But if your character is named Kittamontazimble, you've got to make him (or her?) awfully convincing.

I have often been asked how to present historical facts in such stories, since the group of characters acting out your story may not be aware of the larger turns of history going on about them. I had to solve this problem in *Step to the Music*, where certain battles and events of the Civil War had to be mentioned in order to give the reader a feeling of what was happening, even though my heroine might not be aware of these things at the time. I used the device of opening certain chapters outside my heroine's viewpoint. Here is an example:

> June was hot and long and during its course Staten Island burst into a buzzing place of military camps. Uniforms were to be seen everywhere and the island began to experience its

first trouble with undisciplined soldiers. The *Gazette* carried accounts of drunken assaults on the street, thievery, and vandalism. The old sleepy days were gone and roads bore the new ruts of cannon wheels, the hoof marks of cavalry. Because of the camps, visitors poured in by the hundreds, and on Sunday dust hung like a pall over roads where loaded stages rolled.

In the next paragraph I slipped back into the heroine's viewpoint and stayed there for the rest of the chapter. This technique will also give you time transitions, and even cover distant events. But don't weave back and forth during the course of a chapter, or you will confuse the reader.

STORIES OF OTHER LANDS

Under this heading we should list not merely stories of other lands, but those of the many communities in our own land. Whatever your background, it may be "another land" to someone, and worth writing about. You should be steeped in the country or community about which you write. Often this can be done through research. Of course it is still better to know the community about which you write. In stories for younger children, surfaces may be lightly touched, but something more solid is required as the writer plunges deeper into a real understanding of a life that is different from ours.

Today, however, it is not merely the differences which are emphasized. The lesson every editor is anxious to convey is that under the superficial differences, all races, all peoples are kin. Pearl Buck, out of her knowledge of China, has written a number of books for the 8-10 group which make Chinese children thoroughly real to American boys and girls.

A boy's desire to fly in a plane is not common only to Chinese boys like her hero in *Yu Lan, Flying Boy of China*. Boys all over the world will understand that longing very well. The unhappiness of a little American girl and her Chinese friend who get lost is understandable to any girl anywhere, as is the longing of a girl for a sister, instead of so many brothers. These two situations enter into *The Dragon Fish*.

Florence Crannell Means has written with deep sympathy of American Indians. She has written of the American Negro in *Shuttered Windows* and *Great Day in the Morning*, and of our Japanese-Americans in her courageous *The Moved-Outers*.

A word should be said about the use of dialect in writing about other countries and communities. The wise way to accomplish this is to use idiom rather than dialect. Transpose the order of your words, rearrange sentence structure, use phraseology common to the community about which you are writing, but *don't* use contractions, odd spellings and the like. They are hard on the eye and are enough to discourage most young readers from finishing a story. Readers who live in that community may read the story easily because they know how your queer spellings sound when spoken. But the outsider has no idea and may spend so much time trying to figure out what your character is saying that the effect of your story may be completely wasted.

Much as I admire Lois Lenski and the fine work she has done in writing and illustrating for young people, I must point out that a great many children of my acquaintance find *Bayou Suzette* and *Strawberry Girl* difficult reading because she has made use of actual dialect—contractions and the misspellings of words to imitate the pronunciation of her characters. If you know how Cajuns sound, you can read their dialogue with comfort. If you don't, you are likely to flounder hopelessly.

Here is a bit of Davie's dialogue in William MacKellar's *Wee Joseph:*

> "Aye, it's a grand dog he is for certain, Mr. Blaikie," he agreed. "Will you look at the rare markings on him? I'm thinking there will not be many like him in these parts."

Only a few lines, but we have been given the flavor of the Scottish tongue.

There is a real need today for the story of foreign lands, but the standards are high and you must know whereof you speak. A device I have found useful in writing about another country is to use as my main character an American boy or girl visiting in that country. Then the viewpoint can of course be my own and I can write more soundly out of my own knowledge as a visitor. In both *Secret of the Samurai Sword* and *Mystery on the Isle of Skye* the viewpoint and many of the things seen and experienced are basically the author's, though of course incorporated in a completely fictional story. This device also has the advantage of helping to bridge the gap between the American reader and the foreign characters in the story. The reader can step across more easily if he is viewing the strange scene through American eyes.

Of course I don't mean to imply that the truly foreign viewpoint story isn't wanted as well. But then you must know the country and its people extremely well.

The Modern American Story

This is probably the most popular category of all today. In the beginning, whatever age you write for, if you choose this type of story, you will make acceptance easier for yourself. Modern stories for all ages are wanted and the choice of subject matter is as wide as the American horizon. No problem is too insignificant to write about, no problem is too big and grave, providing youthful interests are considered.

Childhood difficulties that may seem of no real consequence to us as adults may be enormously important to the child who faces them. A story that helps by telling him (indirectly) that he is not alone, that other children have experienced just such problems and come through them satisfactorily, has an important place in today's reading. Such stories always have a sure and easy appeal and many of them are the "light fiction" of the juvenile field. On the other hand a gifted writer may deal with everyday problems with real perception and depth. Such a writer can make the trite story of a girl going to a dance say something important about life and the business of growing up.

At the other end of the scale is the story for young people which deals with wider, grimmer problems. These may be stories of delinquency, or prejudice, stories of the ills of our world and what can be done about them as far as the individual is concerned. The emphasis here needs to be on a positive approach. It is not, I think, a Pollyanna approach, but a realistic one which faces difficulties, but refuses to give up hope. There are no beatniks writing for children.

Certainly an unbalanced diet of sweetness and light is unhealthy for any child. As Josette Frank says in *Your*

Child's Reading Today—a book no writer for young people should miss: "The overprotected child is doomed to bitter disillusion on the inevitable day when he discovers that life is not as it was in his sterilized juvenile reading. And children need to know the evil as well as the good. In the elemental drama of life there is a place for the villain as well as the hero."

Modern stories may be further broken down into separate categories of specialization, and there are some writers who confine themselves to one type of story for all their writing lives. This would not be for me, as I feel that occasional change and experiment is good for the imagination and is more apt to keep the writer from going stale. The following categories are some of the possible breakdowns in this group.

SPORTS STORIES

Sports stories are usually written for older boys, with a few appearing for younger ages. Some girls read these books too, and there are a few swimming, tennis, skiing and other sports stories written primarily for girls. In the latter group Amelia Elizabeth Walden has done an outstanding job of combining the teen-age love story for older girls with an outdoor background. But for the most part men writers have this field to themselves. You'll find sports stories by the score on your library shelves.

As writers of these stories have confessed to me, they are beset by difficulties. Finding new ways to make a basketball or baseball or football game an interesting part of a significant story grows increasingly difficult when so many stories of this sort have been written. Most of the things worth saying about being part of a team have already been said, and you need to play a new variation of the old tunes.

Fortunately human beings have infinite variety and when you start with an individual and well-rounded character he is likely to lead you to a story that is particularly his own.

John Tunis has combined sports and a story of prejudice defeated in his classic, *All-American*. In *Hard to Tackle* Gilbert Douglas writes not only of football, but of a Negro family's struggle to find a decent home in a small town.

It seems advisable these days to add some outside element to your sports story if you are to turn out something that isn't just run-of-the-mill. But any such problem must be well integrated and never a forced issue.

ADVENTURE

Again, these stories are written mainly for boys, though girls often enjoy them, too. The category allows for more variation than the sports story and there can be an imaginative branching out to encompass any sort of action story in any part of the country. Or any part of the world, for that matter.

Since there are fewer limitations in the adventure field, books of greater significance often appear under this heading. In *Hard Nose* Gilbert Douglas has combined adventure and sport in a story of high school football and mountain adventure that has something of real value to say to boy readers. The adventure element is outstanding. The stories of Jim Kjelgaard are especially noteworthy in this field.

MYSTERY

Both boys and girls are always asking for good mystery stories, and editors are always looking for them. Approach the mystery story warily, however, for it is difficult to do well. Too often writers who attempt this type of story for young people become so intent on excitement that they forget that here, too, significance is important. The mystery is a fairly artificial form and it is difficult to tie it logically into a child's world. If you write just another faked and forced mystery, librarians will turn thumbs-down, and no writer can afford that loss of sales. If, however, you can write plausible mystery stories which also have some worth as young people's reading, you will be welcome in either the magazine or the book field.

Certain taboos must be watched. Most of the exciting devices used by the adult writer of mysteries are to be avoided. No dead bodies may be strewn around the scene, and there can be no exceedingly neurotic characters, or vicious crimes. Indeed, it is better to avoid crime of any sort. If you have children mixed up with the capturing of criminals, even though they may have adult help, you're off on the wrong foot.

Since I have made something of a specialty of this field, I can assure you that it is very hard going to work out credible, yet exciting stories in which the mystery is held at the young reader's level, and is not something belonging mainly to the adult world.

Much reading is indicated in this field and again your librarian will help you. The rewards are excellent if you can write really good mysteries.

SCHOOL

These stories are usually combined with some other category, such as sports, romance, mystery, etc., but with special emphasis on everyday school life. To write them, you'd better go back to school for a while yourself, sitting in at a few classes, talking to young people and teachers, wandering the corridors, attending after-school meetings and so on. Just remembering your own school days is not enough.

There is always a ready market for the good school story. Young people of every age like to read about themselves and the everyday problems they face with schoolmates and teachers, from kindergarten on.

HOBBY STORIES

These are sure-fire in both the magazine and book fields, though you are likely to find more examples in the shorter form. Your choice of subjects is as boundless as the horizon. I have written stories of stamp collecting, shell collecting, the making of model planes, and so on. The hobby need not be yours. You can get a lot of story ideas just by investigating some hobby you have known nothing about before.

There is much overlapping in these categories, of course.

One special advantage of the hobby story, and one that makes it popular with editors is that it often gives the reader something to take away and use in his own life. I recall a book by Thelma Harrington Bell called *Captain Ghost*, in which some children find a fallen tree lying beside a fence, and see in it a ship in full sail. The mystery in the story is more or less incidental—the important thing is the way the children, with the help of an elderly sea captain, turn that log into a make-believe ship.

The hobby story, too, can stretch the imagination and arouse an eagerness to do, to create.

It is not necessary to draw any fixed boundaries. I am merely trying to suggest fields which may interest you.

VOCATIONAL

Since this was for a time my own field, perhaps I can be forgiven for talking about it at some length. The vocational novel, or career book, is perhaps the baby of the group. Only in modern times has it achieved popularity and its place in the sun is still challenged by many critics. Unfortunately, the term "career book" has come to carry a slighting connotation because of a serious damage which has been done in this field.

Having discovered that a story which tied in with job information can be very popular with young people (particularly in the girls' field), publishers began reaching out for job stories of all sorts. In some cases, looking first for information, they assigned the writing of these books to authorities in every line except that of writing. The result was an avalanche of books by airplane stewardesses, fashion designers, advertising copywriters, opera stars, in fact members of almost any profession you could name except authorship.

These books, while thick with information that made them blue prints for working at some job, were badly put together, as was natural enough, since the writing of a book is not something to be picked up overnight. The characters were mere names which walked and talked, but bore very little resemblance to real life, and the emotional effect which a valid story should carry was completely absent. Because of the way these badly written books flooded the market, all books which dealt with jobs came to be regarded with suspicion, and those of us who believe in the importance of work in today's world and hope to say something significant on the subject have had a hard pull.

It is my belief that these books can be of real significance and importance, that they can do more toward helping young people to adjust their lives satisfactorily than almost any other type of story. Of course, a good career book should not be limited in its scope to a job alone. All life can come into it, just as life very assuredly comes into every job. There must be, as is true of all the above categories, significance in the writing. The author must have something to say and he must know how to say it in good story-telling form.

ROMANCE

While this, too, may be included in other categories, it is important enough to warrant special attention. Girls from twelve up are the large audience for these books. A touch of romance may be found at times in boys' books, but it is still exceptional. I have heard from librarians that boys will occasionally take out girls' books, if the jackets aren't too drippy. And why not, when so much is to be learned about teen-age boy-girl problems by reading them?

There are perhaps two types of romantic novels. There is the story where romance is treated with a light, gay hand, and the tears aren't too serious. In these stories physical demonstrations of affection are held to a minimum and are of a casual type.

Then there is the more serious novel which may treat

gravely of problems that young people face. Here the author goes much farther toward presenting the truth realistically, and the counselling is often wise and perceptive, presented through the characters as they learn and grow. You must have something worth saying and be able to say it well to write this sort of story. The sensational is not acceptable and good taste is a necessity. In any sort of story in which mistaken conduct is presented so that the characters may learn and arrive at a wiser course, there is always the danger of making the inadvisable behavior (such as racing souped-up cars) seem much more attractive than the sounder road you want to persuade the reader is the right one. Be on your guard against this pitfall.

These more serious books may use a high school or college background, or they may show young people at their first jobs, or even concerning themselves with marriage.

SERIES BOOKS

We cannot close the chapter without considering this category, although for the most part it is outside the fictional concerns of this book. At least some clarifying of the confusing term is possible.

A decade or so ago the "series" referred to fiction such as *The Bobbsey Twins, Tom Sawyer, Judy Bolton* and many others. These stories concerned themselves with the continuing adventures of one set of characters and the emphasis was on action. These books, many of them still published, are produced in quantity and are less expensively priced than the regular trade book. Many of them are frowned upon by librarians as being poor in quality. In some cases the author's name is merely a house name and a stable of writers turns out the books for flat sums and no royalties. Margaret Sutton, however, has always written *Judy Bolton* and has made a very good thing out of that young lady's career.

While this type of series book is still being written, today the name refers mainly to a new type of book for children that came into being not so many years ago, and which now threatens to swamp the market.

The *Landmark Books* serve as a good example, though there are now many other such series. One may deal with historical American figures, another with science, religion, medicine, and so on. A series of well-known *First Books* covers everything from dinosaurs to diamonds. For the most part, these books are non-fiction, though often fiction techniques are used in the writing. They may of course be fictionized biography.

Young people have an apparently insatiable appetite these days for what is "really true," and adults have been quick to draw on the numerous titles now produced in series to feed this hunger.

The field is rather a specialized one, with its own methods of publishing and payment that are outside the province of this book. If you are interested, explore the field through your library and write to the editors.

The listings in this chapter are not by any means complete. I have merely attempted to suggest a reading approach which you can further develop yourself. The technicalities of writing these various types of stories can be learned in part by going to the books. The main story-telling principles remain the same in every case, regardless of how you may specialize.

XIV

The Full-Length Book

It is much more fun to write books than it is to write short stories. The gruelling part of writing anything is working out the plan. That is the difficult, creative part. True, it takes longer to plot a book than it does to plot a short story, but once you have your book plan worked out, your way is fairly simple. Your work schedule stretches ahead of you for several months and you know exactly where you are going. You don't have to think up an entirely new plot every few days as you must when you are writing short stories.

Nevertheless—and though I've said this before, I want to repeat it—you will write far better books if you ground yourself thoroughly in the writing of short stories first. The short story is the more difficult form; once you've conquered it you have the groundwork laid for writing books. The first attempt to change from short story writing to book writing may be a little frightening, however.

Some writers never succeed in the book field because they allow the size of the task to frighten them off. They may start a book, even two or three books, but somehow they never get around to finishing them. The prospect of looking 60,000 words or more in the eye leaves them fearful of their ability to complete the job. If sheer quantity of words terrifies you, try looking at just one chapter at a time. Suppose your chapters run about 3,000 words each and you plan to write twenty chapters. If you write one chapter a week for twenty weeks you will have a book. And what is so frightening about that?

I am going to tell you how I work out a full-length book. Because this is *my* way I like it, but it is up to you to remember that no one writer's way is *the* way. There are probably as many methods of working as there are writers and it is best to find the way most comfortable for you. The house-building analogy I used a few chapters back is all very well as far as it goes, but it is not a perfect analogy. The building of a house is an exact science. It is a manual affair. The writing of a story or a book is psychological. A great deal of blue printing and technical planning may be done, but in the final reckoning it is a thing of the mind and the emotions. Try to the best of your ability to condition yourself in the beginning to sensible, efficient working habits, but if any plan restricts *you,* if the effort to fit yourself to someone else's working method results in inhibiting your imagination—you must go your own way and listen to your own voices.

This is perhaps a dangerous thing to say because it will be to your greatest advantage if you discipline yourself to accepting certain edicts of technique. I am not anxious to offer an easy excuse to the young writer who feels he knows it all when he has learned very little about putting a good story together. It may be a temptation to say, "Ah, but these irksome matters are restricting my creative processes and I'll be better off to go my own way." Don't say that too quickly if you want to sell what you write. But once you have learned the fundamentals of telling a good story, then work out your own manner of getting that story written.

Find out how other writers work. Adapt what you can from their methods and discard whatever seems to restrain you too greatly.

When I am about to launch myself into the writing of a book, I break my writing period of six months into sections of two months each. The boundaries of these sections are not absolutely fixed, but I attempt to fit the progress of my book roughly into three two-month periods. Many writers take much too long to finish a book and I think it is nearly always because they do not arrange some such working schedule ahead. A schedule that will keep them constantly faced with the ominous passing of time. If you can really afford to take from one year to several to write a book, that is your affair. But if you hope to earn a living from your books, you will have to do better than that.

Separate duties are assigned to each of the three sections. The first two months I spend planning the book. The second two are given over to writing it. The third to re-writing, polishing, and typing the final draft.

The planning of a book, though lengthier and more complicated, is not so very different from the planning of a short story. You are going to have more time to develop character, you are going to bring in many more situations and scenes, but you will do a great many of the same things you did in the shorter length. You had better begin by deciding upon your theme, upon the point you want your book to make. Get that down in one sentence and thereafter see that all your material moves the story toward a climax which will prove (as far as your story goes) the thesis you have chosen. If you have been writing short stories you may be faced with a feeling that you must pad in order to eke out sufficient words.

That, in order to fill up all those blank pages, you must bring in everything but the kitchen stove. If you do, you will have a cluttered story which darts in so many directions that no one will know exactly what the book is about.

I learned a sad lesson with the publishing of *The Silver Inkwell*. I thought I had done a neat job of tying all my side issues neatly together to contribute to the whole. The story was (I thought) about a girl who wanted to be a writer and the point I wanted to make was that successful writers do not write from an ivory tower, but from life. When the reviews began to come in I found that each reviewer was looking at a different story. One thought the book was about the publishing business. Another spoke of the juvenile delinquency angle. Some of them even mentioned that it was about writing. What I had done, of course, was to scatter my shots so that few readers could decide just what I was trying to say in the story.

Once you know what your book is to be about, get to work on your outline. Get a looseleaf notebook and make a list of Roman numerals from I to XX. These represent your approximate number of chapters if you intend to write a 50,000 word book. Leave a few lines of space between each number. In these twenty spaces jot down in a very few words what *might* happen in each of those chapters. At the start you may be able to make notations in no more than two or three spaces. Perhaps you know vaguely what your opening scene may be, or that halfway through the book such-and-such will happen, or that your climax will be thus-and-so. If you know anything at all about that story, jot it down in the approximate space where it might occur.

Every day you are going to your desk for a certain period

of time and you are going to play around with that story. In another section of your notebook you are going to introduce yourself to your characters and you are going to work on them every day, too, until you really get to know them: their names, appearance, history, characteristics. You are going to keep some pages free for unrelated ideas which may come to you any time at all. They may not fit into your skeleton outline, since you are not after detail in that, but get them down anyway and elaborate on them when they interest you. Get everything that occurs to you down on paper where it won't get away. There is nothing more maddening than to think of a wonderful idea on Tuesday and have it escape by Saturday because you didn't get it down.

Meanwhile, think, think, think. Train yourself to use every spare minute during the day to pore over some angle of your growing plot. Think about it before you go to sleep at night, not to the point of keeping yourself awake, but to the point where your subconscious is made aware that it had better come up with some contributions if ever it is to be left in peace again.

Chapters of your book may be regarded in the same light as separate scenes of a short story. Each will contribute as a whole to the major problem of the book. Each will have some minor contributing problem which reaches a climax toward the end of the chapter, whereupon it may be resolved and will then give way to a new problem, or meet with defeat, forcing your hero to seek some new way of achieving his aim, or be carried unsolved over to the next chapter.

Be sure you know exactly what problem your hero must work out. In a book the problem need not be made absolutely clear in the first chapter. It may only be hinted at, while the protagonist struggles with some minor story problem, but eventually, as you build up situations and character action, the problem will be revealed in full.

There is one fault to be found more often than any other in the book manuscript of the novice writer. The plot structure is weak. The writer thinks that because he has strung together a number of incidents about the same people, loosely connected in a chronological manner, he has a plot. Of course he hasn't. All he has is a string of incidents loosely strung together in a chronological manner.

Try to see your chapters running along like a series of Japanese boxes. You start with the smallest, lead into the next size, and the next, until you come to your big box, the climax. Each box fits neatly into the following one and the whole belongs together. If you take away any box in the chain and push the rest together they no longer fit. There is a vacant place and you have a rattle. The series is not perfect unless every box is in its proper place.

But your stringer-together-of-incidents has a different set-up. His boxes are all of one size stretched out in a row. Take one away and push the rest together and there is no gap, nothing is missed. There is no inevitable leading from one box to the next as must be the case in a well-plotted book. The climax has not grown step by step from the first chapter, predestined, immutable.

In *Willow Hill* perhaps more than in any other book I have written I was dealing with a single, overpowering problem: how to bring together the young people, white and Negro, in a town torn apart by racial intolerance. That problem could not be thrust into the opening chapter, lest it frighten away the very readers I wanted to reach. Racial understanding is an idea and it does no good to fling ideas at people first. It is an idea which connects strongly with varying sets of emotions, some extremely antagonistic. Therefore I had to approach my subject quietly, carefully, through easily understood sensations and emotions, until the idea could be presented in full force and would carry with it an emotional punch.

The immediate interest of my heroine, Val Coleman, in the first chapter has, on the surface, nothing to do with a racial problem. A boy is coming to live at her house—a boy she has never met. Her best friend, Judy, has annexed a boy friend in Tony Millard, the most popular boy in school. Will the newcomer, Stephen Reid, prove attractive? Will he like Val?

I was writing for teen-age girls, and I knew many of my readers would have no immediate personal interest in racial understanding. But they would be interested at once in a new boy friend. Nevertheless, the gong that is to ring out resoundingly in the climax is lightly touched in that first chapter; touched and stilled at once. In the opening scene at the dinner table Val's mother is perturbed because a housing project for Negroes is being built at the foot of the hill near their house. She is going to a meeting of her women's club that night where the matter is to be discussed. Val is in no wise interested (as the reader is probably not interested) but the first note on the gong has been sounded.

There are various problems and counter problems: at first of interest to girls in general, then, as the reader grows to like Val, of special interest to this particular girl the story is about. Because of the knitting together (by dint of much toil on the part of the author) all these counter problems dovetail and lead into the one smashing problem that makes the achieving of racial understanding in the high school and in the town a matter of major importance to Val and the other young people in the book. If the reader's interest is sufficiently aroused, and her own emotions become involved because of sympathy for the characters, then she will be in an emotional state to accept and understand the idea behind the book by the time she reaches the climax scene.

You can make your plot dovetail by having every character connect in some way with the main problem. Stephen Reid, the new boy, has grown up in a family where racial understanding is regarded as a life-necessity if the world is to survive. He is able to answer Val's doubts wisely and because she likes and respects him, she listens. Val's mother is on the other side in the beginning because of the intolerant woman who heads her club. Judy's boy friend, Tony, is a star basketball player, but his father is Wayne Millard, the town's leading businessman and very much against the opening of the project. Judy and Tony quarrel, and Tony looks in Val's direction in order to spite Judy.

Val is trying for the editorship of the school paper, only to lose out to Mary Evans, who better deserves the post. Mary Evans is a Negro girl and intolerant of white people. Her brother Jeff is an outstanding basketball player, and Tony Millard finds that his desire for a winning team is at odds with his father's interests. Val's father is the high school basketball coach and he doesn't care if a player is pink or green or polka-dotted if he's good with a basketball, and he won't listen to his wife's demands that he put Jeff off the team because he is a Negro. On every hand you have antagonisms, conflicting purposes, and trouble, trouble, trouble. But the contributing problems tie in with the interests of the young girl heroine. There are dates and dresses and games and youthful ambitions. Each contributing problem, though often frivolous on the surface, leads into the main problem which the book is about.

I had a real difficulty on my hands when it came to the handling of the big basketball game. Remember what I told you way back about having the utmost in trouble threaten just before your climax, and then having the trouble *really happen?* I was so tired of reading young people's books where the big game is the climax of the story and the *right* team wins. I wanted to see one book published where the right team would lose and yet the reader would be left satisfied at the end of the story.

Everything depends on the winning of this basketball game. From the point of view of Val and her friends it means disaster for the school and the town if the Willow High team loses, and it means personal disaster for the main characters as well. So—the team loses, the very worst happens.

When I was working on the manuscript I took time every evening to read what I had written out loud to my eleven-year-old daughter. When the Willow High team lost the game she went to pieces over it. "Mother, you can't do that!" I was told frantically. "It's awful! Now you'll never be able to end it. Everything's all wrong. How *will* you end it?" This was something of a poser, but I felt that there was a greater triumph to be worked out than the mere winning of a game, and though my daughter has never forgiven me for leaving her in suspense at that point until I wrote the rest, she feels that the following chapter resolves everything in the most satisfactory way possible.

The outcome, the ending of the story, is something toward which the reader moves from chapter one, and there are no incidents along the way which could be left out without breaking the chain.

As the days go by (keep your eye on the clock and the calendar—you have only two months for this preparation) your skeleton outline will begin to fill up. As the story takes shape you will find some juggling necessary. This incident which seemed in the beginning to fit in best here, now proves to belong somewhere else. Juggle to your heart's content. The more experimenting you do, the more likely it is that you will come up with the best possible arrangement of your material.

And now you can get seriously down to developing your chapter outline in as much detail as you like. Write the numeral I in the middle of the first page of your notebook (all this other doodling has been going on in the back of the book) and set down whatever you know about that first scene. Because of the way you have been working with your material, much of this scene should be easy to outline. In fact, you may work out several scenes with ease. Sooner or later, however, you stick. When that happens, beware!

The moment your imagination balks you are likely to become very tired of all this silly outlining. You know by now just what form your story will take (or think you do) and you feel you might as well start writing. You sit down at your typewriter and sail in. The writing comes with some ease and you feel very pleased with yourself. Now you are Writing a Book. A pricking of conscience reminds you that at Chapter VIII there is a blank space and you don't know what is going to happen at that point in your story. But Chapter VIII is way ahead and you're sure to think up something by the time you get to it.

Anyway, that's what you will assure yourself as you write merrily ahead. But by the time you get to Chapter VIII you find you are just as thoroughly stuck as you were in the outline. Only now it is much more serious because it means breaking the rhythm of your writing. You now have to stop and *think* again. You have to struggle through that difficult spot somehow and it would have been much better if you had listened to no siren voices, but had stayed with the problem while it was still in outline form. Often, when you force yourself to write ahead at this place, you find later that all your work must be done over because it was not sufficiently thought out in the first place.

No matter how difficult the going when you are working on your outline, you will save time and stress and drudgery if you will think your story through completely before you begin writing it.

The treatment to be applied when you reach that place in your outline where you can't think of an idea to fill in, is to get out and feed your imagination some new impressions. If you are writing about a locale which it is convenient to visit, go out and soak yourself in its atmosphere. You'll find answers you could never dream up sitting at home at your typewriter. Or, quite often, you can get yourself out of the knot by reading books of the type you're trying to write. It is not a matter of lifting ideas from another writer, but something more subtle than that. Often, as I read a book which may deal with a subject unrelated to the one I am writing about, some twist the writer may use, some problem which arises, will throw that electric switch in my imagination and suddenly the ideas pour in. Oddly enough, they are not likely to resemble the ideas of the writer whose book I was reading. It is a matter of applying the proper stimulation which will stir up an imagination gone stubbornly sluggish.

It is better to be stymied for days or weeks on your outline than to start writing too soon and be stymied in the same way on the actual writing of the book. If you follow through with your outline then the writing itself will give you no great trouble, because the really difficult work will be behind you.

Let us say, however, that you have been a good little writer and worked your outline through completely from the first scene to the last. Let us say that you have managed by stern discipline to get this done in two months and are now ready to begin the writing of the book.

This is where you clear the decks for action. This is where you cross your friends off your list, behave rudely to anyone who calls you up during your working period, shut the door on salesmen and become anti-social. If you can't be tough enough to do all this, you might as well accept the fact that you are going to dabble at this book for months, perhaps years to come, and that the longer this period runs, the more likely you will be to stack up odds against finishing it at all.

I have spoken earlier in this book about setting a definite wordage schedule in your writing. In the case of the book length piece, this is especially important. I am not one of those writers who can work all day, or even all night on one piece of work. Morning happens to be the time I work best. During a stretch of three or four hours I can comfortably turn out eight pages of 250 words to a page. That amounts to about 2,000 words. By pressing myself, I can do ten pages, or 2,500 words in that time. On rare occasions when a scene so grips me that I am writing at unusually high speed, I can write twelve or more pages.

For my work calendar I take a sheet of paper and write a column of dates on it running on for two months from the time I plan to start writing the book. As I do a considerable amount of lecturing, and have other work on my hands, all of these days will not be open for writing. (Someday I am going to throw everything else overboard and "have time to write!") I compare my schedule of unavoidable engagements with my work calendar and leave those dates blank on which I know I have to be out. I try to get in a five-day writing week, which usually means that I have to work on Sundays, too. Of course there are no "holidays" except Christmas. Even if you have seven days a week on which to write, it may be wise to ask yourself to give no more than five or six days to the job. Then, when the unexpected occurs and you lose a day, you have an extra to fall back on in which you can make up lost ground.

Opposite each date I write the page number and the number of words I should have reached by that date. This is where the psychology comes in. If I press myself too hard and fall short of my schedule, it is easy to become so discouraged that I would turn out less work, instead of more. To avoid this, I require of myself only my "easy" wordage of eight pages a day. But, unless the going is very bad, I do not stop at eight. I push on two more pages and make it ten. Then at the end of my morning's work I enter in red figures, opposite the black ones of my schedule, the wordage I have actually reached on that date. Being ahead of schedule gives me a wonderful feeling of confidence, especially as I see the margin of advantage growing with every day of work. My work schedule will then look something like this:

(Where I should be)	(Where I am)

May

	(Where I should be)			(Where I am)		
Mon. 6	P. 8,	2000	words	P. 10,	2500	words
Tues. 7	P. 16,	4000	"	P. 20,	5000	"
Wed. 8	P. 24,	6000	"	P. 30,	7500	"
Thurs. 9						
Fri. 10	P. 32,	8000	"	P. 40,	10,000	"
Sat. 11	P. 40,	10,000	"			
Sun. 12				P. 50,	12,500	"

On Thursday I knew I would be out and expected no work to be done. On Saturday I got lazy and fell behind. On Sunday I made up for my backsliding, though my schedule required nothing of me that day. The point is that when you have actual figures before you and can see how one day of lost work can throw you behind by a whole 2,000 words at once (if that happens to be your wordage rate for a day's work) you are much more anxious to keep that column of red figures ahead in its race with the black.

In ten working days I can be twenty pages ahead of schedule, and if I could hold to this straight through I could finish the required 250 pages in twenty-five working days, or thirty-five days, taking into account two days off a week. Unfortunately, I have so far never succeeded in accomplishing this happy possibility.

Somewhere along the line something happens to production. I come to a place where everything sticks. The story and characters are so much dust, I am bored to distraction with them, my early delight with the story has faded out. I can see that some of my rosy plans are not taking shape as I had hoped, that much of what I have written is wrong and will have to be done over. The place where this happens is, of course, the place that has been weak all along in my outline. Somehow I have been trusting to luck to discover the answer when I reached that point in the story, but when I do reach it, I find that it sticks more thoroughly than ever and that what I am writing is drivel. The consciousness of the scenes behind me which must be changed begins to weigh heavily and I have the feeling that if I could only get that first part into better shape I would be able to go on.

Opinion differs on what to do at this point. There are writers who say you should push on at all costs. Get it done —no matter how—before you turn back to revise. The danger of going back before you are through is that you may find yourself revising for months or years to come, without finishing the book at all. This may be a very real danger. Particularly with a first book, where the writer is not yet sure whether he can really write that many words. I know several writers who have yet to finish their first books because of this very difficulty.

In my own case, however, I have learned from practice that this is the place for me to turn back for a period of a week or two and reread and revise what has gone before. I doubt if any outline can be completely foolproof. When you get the actual story and characters coming to life, ideas will appear which did not show in the outline and you may very well discover better approaches than you were able to devise in the first place. Don't let these ideas carry you away from the necessary boundaries of your story, but by all means make them welcome where they can be used.

While I am writing ahead on a book and keeping up to schedule, I make the rule never to turn back and reread, except for work done the day before. By reading over the last pages I have written I get into the mood again and regain the momentum which stopped when I put the manuscript aside. Farther back than yesterday's work, however, I do not go at this time. Just as I put my short stories away to "set" for a while before I read them again, I want the early parts of my book to become unfamiliar to me so that I can read them with a fresh eye later on. Of course, through no rereading at this time, there are always small matters which slip by. There are points I meant to take up later, but forgot about; there are other omissions and duplications. This, however, is not too important and will be caught during revision. If you reread constantly you lose your sense of perspective toward the story and will find yourself unable to judge where you have succeeded and where you have failed.

When I reach the point where everything has gone stale, I put my work schedule sorrowfully aside and go back to reread the book from the beginning. Where changing and rewriting is needed, I do it with some care. If I find that a character with whom I had started out is not going to serve the purpose I expected, I may change him into a different sort of person. If some passages seem slow and dull I cut them out with brutal slashes of my pencil.

All this while, in every spare moment of my day, and again before I go to sleep at night, I ponder the problem of that point in my story where my imagination refused to take fire. I know that the answer will come if I keep working at it. By the time I have brought my revision up to date, I have a feeling of greater confidence in my manuscript. The writing behind me now seems more solidly put together, and through rereading I have gained again the impetus and momentum to carry me ahead. The knot unties itself and away I go.

Of course by this time I have fallen behind on my schedule by a week or more and to continue with that particular schedule would be very bad for my writing morale. So now I work out a new schedule, carrying on from the place where I left off. There may be more than one of these recalcitrant spots where I am forced to turn back before I can go ahead, depending on how firm the ground work of my outline has been. If I have been careless and hasty, I pay the heavy penalty.

While you are writing there are a few helpful points to keep in mind. Have your notebook always at hand, for while you are writing one scene your imagination may prove fertile enough to produce all sorts of ideas for future scenes, or for the improvement of scenes already written. Don't let these get away. Jot them down quickly in crude form and go on with the writing of the current scene.

Another useful device is the old one of stopping your day's work while you are still anxious to write the next page, while you still know what you want to say next. If you write to the end of a chapter, or to the point where you don't know what is coming next, it may be difficult to get started the next day. But if you can pick up in the middle of action which interests you, the first hour of writing will come easier.

Sometimes that first hour can be very difficult to sit

through. You are not in the mood and the words won't come. Your impish helper begins to whisper that this is just one of those days and you might as well give up. This is where discipline comes in and you sit there—no matter what. You may have no more than a half a page to show for that miserable hour, but if you stay with it, you'll get the second wind that always comes when you persist and the words will start flowing. I have had the experience of turning out more words in the last hour than in the first two put together.

Eventually the day comes when you write the last word and rip the last page out of your typewriter with a feeling of triumph. The beastly thing is done and are you glad! If you never look at it again as long as you live it will be all right with you.

This, however, is not the time to go on a vacation. You needed only one month in which to write that book, but you've taken at least two, maybe three. There is still a month or more left of the six months you allowed and tomorrow must see you back at your desk, revising and polishing. There is no one to crack the whip except you, and this is the time to crack it.

I always write everything in duplicate. When I have my first draft finished, I then have a carbon copy of it ready. Every correction or change on the original is carefully made on the carbon as well, so that I have two complete copies. One of them is to send to some long-suffering critic, and this I do post-haste. Perhaps I have already sent part of this off somewhere along the way. While I wait for the shattering comment that is sure to come back, I get busy on further revision that I am able to do myself. This is where I really turn into a drudge. My deadline is staring me coldly in the eye and the minutes are flying by. So now I work all day, and sometimes into the evening. In a sense, revision is not as hard as the first writing. It may be wearying, but it doesn't leave you limp and exhausted as a first writing sometimes can. If your story has come to life for you, you feel occasionally that you are actually living each scene, and that can be strenuous. For that reason I cannot work for a long stretch on first draft material. But rewriting does not take it out of me in the same way and I am willing to crowd that into every minute I can spare.

There is the typing, too—a good two weeks' job in itself. Sometimes I begin typing the first part of a book before the last part has been revised. I envy the writer who sends his stuff off to a typist and washes his hands of it. I don't like to do that because I find a thousand and one small changes to make when I get to the actual copying that I have missed in every other reading.

When the typing is done (I make an original and three copies at the request of my editors), I must read it all again and correct my typographical errors on all copies. Later, along come galley proofs and I read with a sense of nausea. I am so sick of the manuscript that I tell myself I don't care whether it ever sees publication—just so *I* don't ever have to read a word of it again.

But the months go by and publication date rolls around. Along comes a package of books and I break into it with hands that are clumsy because they're shaking a bit with excitement. And there it is—a real live book! *Mine*. Mm, not a bad jacket. Nice illustrations, too. "Whitney" looks impressive on the cover. Of course I am into another book by now and going through the same grief this one has caused me all over again. But for once I throw discipline and 2,500 words to the winds. I sit down in the nearest chair and start reading.

Say—this is good! Did I write this? Somehow it looks and reads a million times better in print than it ever did in manuscript. Clever girl, this Whitney. Can't put her stuff down. What dialogue, what suspense, what emotion! She's actually got me sniffling in the last chapter. And I put the book aside with a sigh. Really, there ought to be more.

My favorite author.

But if I don't get back to work I won't be my favorite author by this time next year.

XV

LETTERS FROM EDITORS

There is one group of critics who can be counted on to be honest—your editors. They have a decided personal interest in getting from you the best work you can do. Theirs is the final judgment before your story sees print. Busy as they are, they are willing to take time every day to write words of criticism to writers who prove they can take it and profit by it. When those letters begin to come your way, treasure them and be guided by them.

Every letter I have received from an editor has been saved. When these began to pile up I got a special scrapbook in which to mount them. This book is one I still thumb through frequently, one that I will always learn from. Even when you know the rules and recognize your own weaknesses, reminders are frequently necessary.

I would like to share with you some of these criticisms I have received from editors. They are worthy of your attention. Not all of them concern stories written for young people, but the comments are applicable to any type of story.

> There is color here and the dialogue is crisp and the story moves, but several things I don't like. Chuck's ruse is not convincing. He doesn't *undertake* anything —but that's the backbone of a good plot. There is too

long an introduction leading up to the problem which is to confront Chuck; the story might very well begin with it. Then it would be motivated.

We have been very much interested in your story, "Black Diamonds," although we consider that our readers might be a little bewildered by the conclusion of it. When there is a "surprise ending" we generally have to plant a few more clues than you have planted here. Our regular subscribers have told us so many times that it isn't fair to fool them.

This is too obviously synthetic. You didn't write it seriously, did you? We don't want realism, of course, but we do want the illusion at least of reality.

Were you sincere when you wrote the last two stories we have seen of yours, or were you deliberately "slanting" the material in our direction? It is almost fatal to do that. The story can hardly fail to sound synthetic, since it's on emotion we depend; and how can you manufacture emotion?

"The Cinnabar Box" seems unconvincingly set forth, and is a bit disjointed. The shifting of viewpoint making it a little hard for the average reader to follow, because the thread of the plot breaks often enough to disturb the train of thought.
A thin line often divides the convincing from the unconvincing. A story must *seem* possible while the reader is reading it; if it does not seem possible, if it is on the wrong side of this thin dividing line, it succeeds merely in being grotesque.

The story of a girl rising above her lack of courage has such a familiar Sunday-school ring that we almost always avoid it. We would not have girls deliberately running the risk of contacting bandits voluntarily either, even as a dare or a school prank.

There is too much background detail and too leisurely an introduction of characters and action. In other words, the characters do not come to life and the story hesitates.

If writers wouldn't use retrospect, they'd be a lot surer fire.

We like this story very much, and we feel sure that it will be popular among our readers. It has an excellent beginning to arouse the interest right away, and the suspense is beautifully kept up throughout the story.

We do not use criminal characters in any of our story papers.

Your introduction of characters is vague because over on page 3 we find that one of the boys is a girl.

"Court of the Magnolias" is such a colorful story and contains such attractive young people that it gives us real pleasure to purchase it.

Because "Stage Fright Cure" treats a problem that is very prevalent we especially regret its unavailability for our paper. Our first requirement of a story is that it be entertaining. A story which lacks that quality will be passed up by the reader. The stage-fright and shyness experiences of most adolescent girls are much too painful to be entertaining. Also, there is too little emphasis on plot. Several pages throughout the story hold up the action for some time.

We are delighted to have had the opportunity of reading your story, "Conch Shell." We like its fine message of tolerance, its unusual setting, and its naturalness of conversation and action.

Because the situation in "The Chance for Nancy" is unpleasant and a little artificial, with its outcome foreseen, we are returning your story.

The plot pattern is fairly familiar, consequently there is little incentive for the reader to go on to a denouement which she has already anticipated. Gwen seems unnaturally sulkish and boorish—much more so than we should like to have one of our characters pictured.

Contrasting views on the same story:
"Meet Miss Jones" doesn't appeal. In the first place, we do not like the hero and get no thrill when the heroine finally secures him.

"Meet Miss Jones" is nicely done and our check is enclosed herewith.

I think it's always a good idea to wait before rewriting—to let your subconscious play with the story idea.

Not enough struggle and conflict in this one.

The heroine is so consistently a pain in the neck during the greater part of the story that her reform at the climax is hard to believe.

Learn your character conflict. Read "Pride and Prejudice" over again. Don't go delving into ancient history for so much of your plot value. The whole first two pages is retrospect and we like our action to be forward.

Following are excerpts from letters written me concerning my first book. It was rejected by three publishers before the fourth bought it. I was so discouraged by the three rejections that I very nearly didn't send it out a fourth time. The moral is obvious. You don't sell stories by putting them away in a file. A rejection may mean only that the story doesn't fit that market.

I have read all of your manuscript, *House of Tomorrow*, and although I do think that you have a splendid idea here and I like the sympathetic, friendly and hopeful way in which you manage it, I do not see a possibility of adding this story to our list in the near future.

We have read with interest your manuscript *House of Tomorrow*. After careful consideration we have decided that we should not undertake the publication of this story.

It was most kind of you to let us see *The House of Tomorrow*, and we have enjoyed our study of it.

We publish a restricted number of juveniles, and we only take on a new author when we feel reasonably certain that we can do well with his work. This story shows promise, but it does not seem sufficiently outstanding to us, and we feel doubtful of its sales possibilities.

We have been reading with quite special interest the script of your *House of Tomorrow*.

Before reaching a final decision we would like to learn from you something about the material upon which your very interesting story is based (if, indeed, it had a foundation in fact), and as much of your own background as you think might help our picture of the book.

In this case the heroine of our story lived happily ever after because the last publisher, Houghton Mifflin, brought out the book under the title, *A Place for Ann,* and the sales achieved refuted the prophecy of another publisher concerning "sales possibilities."

XVI

To Market, to Market!

Now your brain child is groomed and ready to go off and earn her own way. Her hair has been combed and her teeth straightened and you are going to see to it that your offspring will make a good first impression. To accomplish this you have put the little darling's best foot forward on your very first page.

Your manuscript has been typed with ribbon dark enough so that the editor will not need a magnifying glass to figure out what you are trying to say. You have used a paper with a good rag content because that will bear up through several mailings without looking like something just fished from a wastebasket. You have double-spaced, of course, and left margins of an inch or more all around. On the first page you have typed your name and address in the upper left corner, and the approximate number of words in the upper right. For young people's magazines, where you are permitted no great wordage, an exact count won't hurt you with the editor. I don't mean that you need to enter your wordage as "1,834 words." "1,800" will do. But make sure that your rough guess wasn't wrong so that the actual count runs 2,000.

A third of the way down the page you have written your title in caps, two spaces lower the word "BY" and beneath that the name under which you choose to write. Count your spaces so that the balance is good and your title heading looks well on the page.

Titles are important, so find a good one, if you possibly can. For young people a title which is concrete and presents some picture is best, rather than the abstract sort of title often found in the adult field. A good story title should sound interesting, it should intrigue at first glance. Of my own book titles, I like *The Silver Inkwell* best, and that was the simplest book to title, since there was an inkwell in the story. Sometimes a title can be a very difficult thing to find. "Storm Over the Art League" was a hard story to title. Neither editor nor author was satisfied with the one finally used, but somehow we could hit on nothing better. An intriguing and challenging title is especially helpful if you are unknown to the editor. It won't sell your story if the rest doesn't match the title, but it is a good way to arrest interest and get your goods into the show window.

If your manuscript is not very long you may fold it three times and put it into a long envelope. Have it weighed for accurate postage and enclose a stamped, addressed envelope. In the case of a longer story, it is better to use large Manila envelopes and mail without folding. You can send a book manuscript cheaply at the Educational Materials rate.

Whether you enclose a letter to the editor depends on whether you have anything of importance to tell him. If you have sold to other markets, that is worth mentioning. But make your remarks as brief as possible. Don't write and tell him how you got the idea for the story, or that it is something which really happened to your great-aunt Martha. He doesn't care. Above all, don't accompany your manuscript with a letter explaining what the story is about. The story itself should take care of that. If it doesn't, you'd better re-write it. And of course don't write to say how much you need the money. (A number of people do!) Bother him as little as possible. If your story is good it will speak for itself.

Before you favor this particular editor with your story, you will have read several issues of his magazine from cover to cover in order not to waste his time and yours by sending him something of a length and type that is entirely unsuited to his use. Simple common sense should tell any writer this, but apparently thousands of beginners send their stories gayly off every day without the faintest idea of the content of the magazines to which they so optimistically mail them.

Know your markets. Read your markets.

This doesn't mean that because you read a camping story in the last issue of *American Girl* you immediately send that editor another camping story. All editors are looking for variety within the scope of their own particular needs. Every magazine has its own flavor and you must learn what that flavor is by reading many issues of the magazine.

Markets change from year to year and your best bet is to keep up subscriptions to one or two good writers' magazines which will keep you posted on changes in editorial policy, and will supply you with the names and addresses of magazines and papers using the type of material you want to write.

In the beginning do not shun the more humble markets in your field. I will be forever grateful for the apprenticeship years I served writing for the pulp paper magazines, and for the training that experience gave me. This sort of writing will never hurt you if in *every story you write you do the very best work you are capable of doing at that time.* If, be-cause the market does not pay very much and you regard it as unimportant, you write carelessly and with indifference, you will be doing yourself a decided injury. And probably you will not sell what you write. Good work cannot be done while you have your tongue in your cheek and are looking down your nose. It is a bitter pill for the vanity of the beginner to take, but it is more than likely that he will be lucky if he is good enough at first to sell to the most humble market.

It is true that badly written, badly put together stories will be found in low-pay magazines, but instead of wasting your time sneering at these stories, set yourself the goal of doing much better. Because someone else does sloppy work doesn't mean that you need to. If you hold to the rule of always trying to better your own record, you will soon write yourself out of the smaller markets.

.For the beginner in the children's field the church-school papers are an excellent training ground. There are many, ranging from those which pay only a few dollars for a story, to those which pay good rates and have high literary standards. Write to your favorite writer's magazine for a back issue which lists these markets. Then write the editors for sample copies.

Sooner or later the question of whether or not to work through an agent comes up. I have never used an agent for selling either stories or books in the young people's field. I have broken into these markets as an unknown, and you can do likewise. As a matter of fact, few agents handle juvenile material, so you might as well be your own salesman to start with. In the case of non-fiction or very specialized material, an agent's advice may be necessary, but for the most part you do not need one until it comes to the matter of secondary rights on book material. Then, if your publisher does not handle these rights through his own agent, you may want to call in someone outside to handle them for you. As a rule, juveniles do little in the radio, movie, or foreign field, but of course yours might be the exception.

Book manuscripts, too, can be sent in "cold" and be assured of a first reading, and a second and more, if deserving of consideration. If you happen to know someone who knows a children's editor, the introduction may help to get you personal attention from the editor-in-chief, but it won't serve to sell a story that editor doesn't want to buy. Your story itself is your salesman. If it is a good story, you need not worry about its finding a place.

In the short story field there are two methods of paying for a story—either on acceptance, or on publication. The better markets pay when your story is accepted, no matter how long it may be held for publication. When it is accepted and paid for, don't expect to see it on the stands the following month. It is far more likely to be a matter of several months before it will see the light in printed form. In the case of small markets which pay on publication, the waiting may be weary indeed, but it is better to be published somewhere, than not to be published at all.

In the book field the matter becomes more complicated, for here you will sign a formal looking contract, the first sight of which may dismay you completely. There are certain things you should know about contracts, though in your first one you may have to take exactly what is offered you. Fortunately all reputable publishing houses have a standard contract which varies very little from house to house.

A 10% royalty on the list price of every copy sold is the usual offer to a new author. Don't accept a set sum without royalty payment unless you have given up hope of having the manuscript taken elsewhere. If the publisher likes your book well enough so that he doesn't want you to take it elsewhere, he may agree to a "sliding scale." If you are courageous enough you can request this to start with. I requested it, but I didn't get anywhere with my request. Once you have shown that you can produce repeatedly and that your books are popular enough to run up sales, you are in a better position to bargain. In the sliding scale the most common practice is to pay the author a 10% royalty up to 5000 copies sold, 12½% to 10,000 and 15% after that. There are variations of this scale, depending on the generosity of the publisher with whom you are dealing and how badly he is in need of authors.

What you receive in the way of an advance usually depends on how much your book is wanted, and how much you need the money. Since an advance comes out of later royalties, you are ahead nothing except in the matter of time. Of course if your publisher is willing to pay you an advance, the money paid will serve as pressure to make sure that he publishes the book with reasonable dispatch in order to get his own investment back. As your success as a writer grows, so does the size of the advance paid you, since it is no longer a gamble as to whether or not your books will sell.

The clause which most irks me in a contract is that which has to do with an option on an author's work. Usually every contract requires that you submit your next book, perhaps your next two books, to that publisher. In other fields of business a sum of money is usually paid for an option, but in the literary field it is not. An option on your next book is something you give the publisher free of charge.

In the case of a first book, where the publisher is taking a chance by publishing it at all, it is only fair that he should have first look at your next book. But he isn't entitled to sew you up for more than one. If you refuse he will probably be satisfied with an option on one.

Options can cause a writer a great deal of grief. You cannot know until you have been through the publishing mill just how matters will work out with that particular publisher. If the set-up proves unhappy, if you feel your book has not been given a sufficient chance to sell, if other matters go wrong, you may not want to have that publisher take your next book. But the option will tie you, willy, or nilly.

Above all, beware of any publisher who asks you to help foot the bill, or to guarantee the sale of a certain number of copies. These are known to the trade as "vanity publishers," since they prey upon the young writer's desire to see his book in print. They operate within the law for they do everything the agreement requires of them. The book is printed (a small number of copies) and it is sent off to reviewers, who ignore it because the imprint of the publisher is in poor repute. There the matter rests and the bewildered author finds that his book is in none of the stores and that it is not selling.

There is a magic word in the book business which means little to the novice, but which is the key to the entire situation. That word is "distribution." If your book does not get into the bookstores—and that doesn't mean just the stores in your home town, but all over the country—it is not going to sell. To achieve good distribution takes a tremendous sales organization and only the big, well-established publishing houses have this force of salesmen covering the country. The vanity publisher has no such force at his command. The way he makes his money is by milching the writer. Bookstore people are a canny lot and they know better than to touch the books of those publishers who require their writers to pay part of the printing expense. If a book is really good, it will sell to a reputable publisher. If the writer has to pay the publishing costs, it usually means that the book was so poor that it could not be published elsewhere.

However, you may not sell your first book to a big house. You may find the competition there too keen for you to break in at once, and it may be wiser to achieve publication by taking your manuscript to a smaller house. The smaller house, as a rule, does not have the distribution enjoyed by a larger firm and consequently does not sell as many copies of a book. Nevertheless, a number of them do a very creditable job. By building up a record of consistent quality behind them they find their books welcome at every store, even though their lists may be extremely small.

Once your book has been accepted and the contract signed, you might as well relax as far as that book goes. Nothing you can do will hurry it into print. At the very least it will probably take nine months to be published, and it is quite likely to take a year or more. Forget about it and get that next book done.

With a first book, the publisher will probably not consult you on the matter of an artist, format, dust jacket, or any of the other things which pertain to the printing end. In all likelihood he knows more about these affairs than you do, and you had better be a well-behaved author and let him alone. Unless you really are an authority, you'd better trust to his judgment. Your book isn't the first he's ever printed. After you have had several published you may get a little more biggety and want a finger in this pie, but in the beginning attend to your own end, which is writing, and let him attend to his.

When the galleys come along, don't go haywire and start rewriting the whole book. There will be a clause in your contract concerning author's corrections and if you make too many you'll be charged for your little whimsies. The time to rewrite is while your book is still in manuscript form, not after it is set up in type, where corrections can be expensive.

Before leaving the subject of marketing your manuscript, either story or book, I want to say something on the subject of taboos in writing for children. This comes under the head of marketing, even though it is a matter you will have to consider at the very beginning when you are planning your story. If you break certain accepted rules you will not be able to sell your manuscript at all. On the other hand, some markets are stricter about these rules than others.

In great part it is a matter of common sense and good taste. Sometimes I've heard people say, "Isn't it difficult to write with all these restrictions and taboos hemming you in?" I don't find it so. If you write wholesome stories about wholesome, attractive young people, the taboos will trouble you very little.

The taboos are a little stricter in magazines than they are in the book field. The church-school papers are most careful, but don't think for a moment that the stories used by the religious market are moralistic and preachy, or even religious. They don't want stories in which young characters smoke or drink—but smoking and drinking are not as a rule necessary to your story, so it is no hardship to omit them. Nor do they want stories about criminals, or frightening stories, or those dealing with depressing subjects. By study-ing the markets you will find what is acceptable in each, and in many cases the paper itself may send you a list of the taboos they like their authors to respect.

In the book field the restrictions are fewer, and more and more old taboos are going into the discard. Until recently stories of handicapped young people would not be accepted. But in a year's time there have been two fine books for older girls in which the heroine was seriously handicapped.

Both *A Cup of Courage* by Mina Lewiton and *Jennifer* by Zoa Sherburne treat the subject of an alcoholic parent with understanding and penetration. The subject of divorce is also used by Mina Lewiton in *The Divided Heart*, the sensi-tive story of a girl torn by her love for both parents.

There have been many books about the adopted child, and several about stepfamily situations. I have written about the latter in *Linda's Homecoming* for the older teens, and for a slightly younger age in *Mystery of the Green Cat*.

We are no longer afraid of dealing with racial problems of all sorts in books for young people. In fact any minority group may be written about providing you know your sub-ject well. I chose Mexican-American migrant workers in *A Long Time Coming*—perhaps an unlikely subject for the juvenile field. Yet the book continues to find a market year after year.

Even sex is no longer wholly taboo, though I don't recom-mend getting too realistic about it in the average teen-age story.

Taboos are being dropped mainly in the older field, and have not by any means been discarded by all publishers. The thing to remember in writing the type of story which has its roots in thoroughly unpleasant realism, is to make the story one of courage and high hope. Then it will be a book to help, rather than to discourage and pain and hurt. Such a story takes upon itself a grave responsibility.

In stories for the younger group, avoid having your hero or heroine set an example which you would not want your young reader to follow. If you write a story about a youngster who runs away from home, don't have everything turn out wonderfully so that other youngsters may want to follow that example.

Above all, don't have your characters in a story do something which might be actually harmful. I remember one book manuscript about which an editor consulted me. It was an interesting, well-written story by a writer who had already had a book published. This one was about a little girl who decided to have a party while her mother was away. She made cookies herself and invited the mailman, the milkman and a door-to-door salesman to the party. She burned the cookies, but the party was a great success and Mother was not particularly disturbed when she came home. If *my* young daughter lighted the stove while I was away and invited the mailman, the milkman and a strange salesman to a party, I'm afraid I would use the hairbrush to good effect. Certainly no book should be published which sets a harmful, even dangerous example, as this manuscript did. To say nothing of the minor point that the milkman, the mailman, and salesman would never in their right minds accept such an invitation while mother was away!

Use common sense in checking your story subject. If you aren't sure, talk to a teacher or librarian, or someone else who can give you good advice.

And now for a few words in conclusion. Perhaps I've made writing sound like very hard work in this book. If I have, it was intentional. It *is* hard work. It is not something to be tossed off easily while the writer sits back and reaps rewards of money and glory.

The early years of every writer are filled with discouragement and despair and disappointment. There is one hopeful thing to keep in mind, however. Progress, apparently, is made in a series of level stretches which can run along for some time before the next level is reached. I have heard artists comment on the same thing. You plod along day after day at one level, with no sign of any improvement or progress. And then one day, almost without realizing it, you have taken a step up and now find yourself on the next higher level. There you will remain for a time before you move up again toward that high state of perfection which will always move on ahead of you like a will-o'-the-wisp, never to be fully grasped. But how disappointing it would be to grasp it fully and have nothing more to try for. How much more fun to always reach out your hand for something still ahead.

Often in the beginning you will say, "If I could just sell *one* story!" Somehow that magic first sale looks like the opening of a wonderful door to a road that will thereafter be easy. It isn't. Sometimes it seems as hard to sell the second, the third and the fourth story as it was to sell the first. Each time you find yourself wondering if you can ever do it again. But if you keep trying, you will.

Despite my wounds and bruises, my head is unbowed and I know that I wouldn't trade my profession for any other profession in the world. A writer's office is under his hat and he can take that hat wherever he chooses to go. He is freer by far than most men in our modern civilization. His eggs need not be all in one basket, and he is hemmed in by no horizons that cannot be changed.

Writers stay young more successfully than other mortals do. Perhaps it is because no man who has a keen and lively interest in life can really grow old. And when you are a writer, your senses never atrophy. Every scene, every person you meet, everything that is said and done around you is grist for your ever-active mill.

Particularly is this true of those who write for children. When you are kept busy seeing everything about you through young, excited eyes, there is no time to be bored. He who is ever interested is ever young.